MM Mount Morris Tour & Historic District

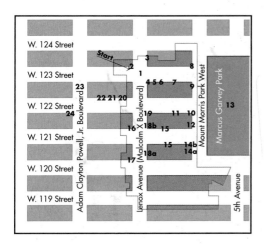

HC Harlem Central Tour & Historic District

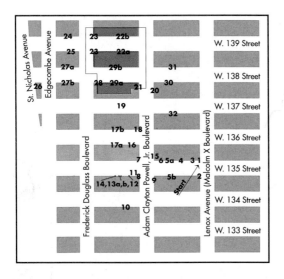

St. Nicholas Avenue

Edgecombe Avenue

24 23   22b   W. 139 Street

25   23   22a

27a   29b   31   W. 138 Street

27b   28 29a   30   W. 137 Street
26   21 20

19

32   W. 136 Street

17b 18

17a 16   W. 135 Street

Frederick Douglass Boulevard

Adam Clayton Powell, Jr. Boulevard

Lenox Avenue (Malcolm X Boulevard)

7   15
          6 5a 4 3 1

11 8   W. 134 Street
14,13a,b,12   9   5b   2

10   W. 133 Street

Start

Hamilton Heights Tour
& Historic District

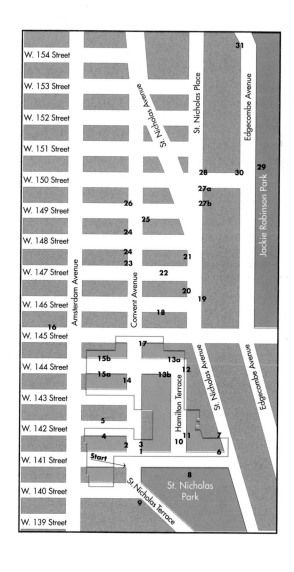

W. 154 Street

W. 153 Street

W. 152 Street

W. 151 Street

W. 150 Street

W. 149 Street

W. 148 Street

W. 147 Street

W. 146 Street

W. 145 Street

W. 144 Street

W. 143 Street

W. 142 Street

W. 141 Street

W. 140 Street

W. 139 Street

St. Nicholas Avenue

St. Nicholas Place

Edgecombe Avenue

Jackie Robinson Park

Amsterdam Avenue

Convent Avenue

Hamilton Terrace

St. Nicholas Avenue

Edgecombe Avenue

St. Nicholas Terrace

St. Nicholas Park

Start

31

28   30   29

27a

27b

26

25

24

24   21

23

22

20

18   19

16

17

15b   13a

15a   14   13b   12

5

4   13b

2   3   1

11   7

10   6

8

9

Jumel Terrace Tour & Historic District

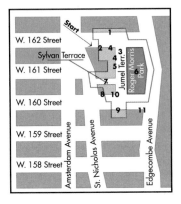

Touring Historic Harlem

Four Walks in Northern Manhattan

Touring Historic Harlem

Four Walks in Northern Manhattan

Andrew S. Dolkart
and Gretchen S. Sorin

New York Landmarks
Conservancy
1997

Contents

This publication was made possible by a grant from American Express Company.

Additional funding was provided by The Greenwall Foundation, the Graham Foundation for Advanced Studies in the Fine Arts, and the Office of Manhattan Borough President Ruth W. Messinger.

The second printing was made possible, in part, by a grant from the Upper Manhattan Empowerment Zone Development Corporation.

Foreword

American Express Company is proud to have supported
Touring Historic Harlem: Four Walks in Northern Manhattan, the
latest title in the Landmarks Conservancy's series of
guidebooks to New York's historic neighborhoods.

From its Dutch origins to its evolution into one of
America's leading African-American communities,
Harlem has an extraordinarily rich architectural and cultural heritage. Authors Andrew Dolkart and Gretchen
Sorin have brought this history to life with a wonderful
series of walking tours which illustrate the development
of Upper Manhattan through its historic buildings and
neighborhoods. Harlem has always had a magic lure.
The authors explain how and why this attraction is so
enduring.

Today, blocks of historic rowhouses, apartment
houses, churches, schools, and commercial buildings
pay tribute to Harlem's past and hold hope for its future.
American Express's support for this guidebook demon-
strates our belief that the preservation of the architectural past enhances our economy and quality of life.

We hope that this guidebook encourages you to
explore Harlem and look carefully at the many fine
buildings which line its streets and boulevards.

Sincerely,

Harvey Golub
Chairman and Chief Executive Officer
American Express Company

Acknowledgements

This walking tour book was completed with the assistance of many people. We would especially like to thank the librarians and archivists at the following institutions who aided our research efforts and our search for photographs: New York Public Library, Schomburg Center for Research in Black Culture; New York Public Library, American History, Local History, and Genealogy Division; New York Public Library for the Performing Arts; New-York Historical Society; New York State Historical Association; Museum of the City of New York; Avery Library, Columbia University; and the Library of Congress. At the New York Landmarks Conservancy, we are grateful for the support of Peg Breen, President and Roger Lang, as well as Amy Lamberti, Ellen Washburn Martin, Philip Norkeliunas, and Jennifer Wellock. Individuals who provided information or advice include Alice Adamczyk, Paris R. Baldacci, Tom Bess, Mary Beth Betts, Ken Cobb, Marsha Dennis, Frank Driggs, Franny Eberhart, Carl Forster, Christopher Grey, Gale Harris, Laura Hansen, Jonathan Kuhn, Deborah McCaffery, Dale Neighbors, Marjorie Pearson, Catherine Raddatz, Steven W. Segal, Jay Shockley, Julie Sloane, Martin Sorin, Anne Steinert, Susan Tunick, Margaret Walton, Stephen Watson, and Wayne Wright. We were lucky to have a number of people who graciously read the text with a critical eye. These included Sandra Griffith, Ken Lustbader, Robert R. Macdonald and our editor Irene Cumming Kleeburg. We especially appreciate the work of Ron Gordon and Abraham Brewster of The Oliphant Press whose design adds special character to the completed project.

Introduction

The Architecture and Development of Harlem

Andrew S. Dolkart

Harlem...no other neighborhood in New York City conjures up such a diversity of images as does this section of northern Manhattan. To many, Harlem is the center of a dynamic community and the heart of a vibrant African-American cultural heritage; others see Harlem as a symbol of urban blight and of the societal failures of America; and to still other people Harlem is a treasure trove of underappreciated 19th- and early-20th-century architecture, especially rich in residential and ecclesiastical buildings. In part, each of these visions is true, for Harlem is an extremely diverse neighborhood with a complex history of development and change.

Dutch governor Peter Stuyvesant established Nieuw Haarlem in 1658 on land comprising most of northern Manhattan. The actual village settlement centered on the Harlem River at about East 125th Street. The village thrived as a social and political center, but most of

Harlem Plain, 1814.

Fifth Avenue looking north from East 118th Street towards Mount Morris Park and its fire watch tower, c. 1880. The sign at the left, advertising for the sale of this property, records the impending demolition of the old wooden houses and the leveling of the rocky outcrop.

Harlem was inhabited by farmers. Since the Dutch were slave owners, Harlem had a substantial African population from the inception of its settlement. In 1666, the British provided Harlem with a fixed southern boundary, drawing a diagonal line across Manhattan Island, running from approximately what is now West 129th Street on the Hudson River to East 74th Street on the East River. The historic boundary was forgotten as Harlem was integrated into the growing city. In fact, as early as 1683 Harlem was considered a part of New York City and County, even though it remained a sparsely populated rural district with none of the character of the burgeoning metropolis at the southern end of the island.

Geographically, Harlem divides into two distinct areas—the Harlem Plain in the central and eastern part of the area and the Heights, formed by the steep cliffs of Manhattan schist, to the west. Contact between Harlem and New York City residents was generally limited to the presence of a number of country estates on the Heights. Most of these were owned by city residents who moved to Harlem in the summer, escaping the heat and the epidemics of the city and taking advantage of the cooling breezes and expansive views on the elevated sites. Two of the estate houses are extant—Hamilton Grange (HH3) and the Morris-Jumel Mansion (JT6).

By the early 19th century, the farmland of the Harlem Plain was deteriorating and many of the farms were abandoned. However, the area retained a rural ambiance and the village continued to prosper. The inauguration of train service along Fourth Avenue (now Park Avenue) by the New York and Harlem Railroad in 1837 had a great impetus on development in portions of Harlem. By the 1860s, many of the streets to the east of the railroad were heavily built up, while wooden suburban homes were scattered elsewhere in the area.

A few shantytowns appeared in the western part of Harlem by the mid 19th century. The shantytown residents were largely Irish, with a smaller number of Germans and members of other groups. A health inspector noted in 1866 that only a Third Avenue railroad car was more densely packed than a shantytown and then described the scene in Harlem in more detail:

> Men, women, and children, dogs, cows, pigs, goats, geese, ducks, and chickens are almost promiscuously mixed together. The street is rank with filth and stench, and the consequence is that mortality holds high carnival there.

Shanties continued to spread throughout Harlem in the post-Civil War decades, until a goat grazing on a rocky outcropping became a standard image of the community. Despite the presence of these shantytowns, much of the area remained vacant and many New Yorker's found Harlem's rural charms inviting, and traveled to the area for picnics and other outings.

As New York City's population grew and as residential development pushed northward on Manhattan Island, the urbanization of Harlem became inevitable. For several decades, speculative development was inhibited by a paucity of commuter transit links between Harlem and the business districts to the south. This changed dramatically between 1878 and 1880 when elevated rail lines penetrated into Harlem along Second, Third, and Eighth avenues. The arrival of the els precipitated land speculation and the start of speculative residential construction.

The metamorphosis of sections of Harlem into prestigious residential communities took place in the late

Eighth *Avenue beneath the elevated, looking north from 116th Street, in 1898.

1880s and early 1890s. Intensive development occurred on the streets to the west of Mount Morris Park, on Convent Avenue and adjacent streets, and in the West 130s between Seventh and Eighth avenues, creating three of New York City's finest rowhouse neighborhoods. This development, and residential construction elsewhere in Harlem, was undertaken almost entirely by speculative builders, most of whom borrowed money to erect houses that were then either sold individually to a prospective homeowner or as a group to a middle man who then sold or rented individual units. In most cases, little-known architects who specialized in speculative rowhouse design were responsible for these buildings, but on occasion a prestigious architect would become involved in rowhouse design, such as Francis Kimball who designed what is perhaps New York City's finest row of Queen Anne houses for a site on West 122nd Street (MM22), and McKim, Mead & White, Bruce Price,

10

and James Brown Lord who were responsible for the extraordinary King Model Houses on West 138th and 139th streets (HC22 and HC29). A few freestanding mansions also appeared in Harlem, notably on the Heights where, for example, circus owner James Bailey erected a spectacular house in 1886-88 (HH28).

The rowhouse builders in Harlem sought to attract middle- and upper-middle-class buyers, with many of the new residents moving to Harlem from neighborhoods south of 59th Street which were experiencing an influx of commercial development or the intrusion of cheap tenements planned to house poor immigrant families. The new homeowners and renters were attracted to Harlem by its quiet ambiance, its abundant park land, and the low cost of housing in comparison to other Manhattan neighborhoods. The vast majority of the new homeowners were American-born, white Protestants, although the area also attracted a significant number of successful immigrants. Households were often fairly large, consisting of the immediate family, extended family members, and one or more servants. Most of the servants were young women, generally recent immigrants from Ireland, although German and Swedish servants

The lowrise character of Harlem is evident in this 1927 view looking north from the Hotel Theresa on Seventh Avenue and 125th Street.

128-134 West
121st Street (Clever-
don & Putzel, 1890-
91) in 1891.

were also common and there were a few instances of
live-in black servants, mostly migrants from Virginia and
Maryland.

Not all of Harlem's new residents lived in single-family houses. Coincident with the construction of rowhouses, a significant number of multiple dwellings were
erected. Some of these, such as the Washington Apartments on Seventh Avenue and West 122nd Street
(MM24), are early examples of apartment houses
designed for middle-class families, while many others
were tenements. These tenements were generally of a
higher quality than those on the Lower East Side and in
other poor immigrant districts, and tended to attract civil
servants, small business owners, and other middle- and
working-class people.

The new residents established institutions in the
neighborhood that catered to their religious and social

needs. Since many of Harlem's inhabitants were quite prosperous they could afford to commission noted architects to erect fine new churches, clubs, and other structures on prestigious corner sites. Harlem's streets are graced with an exceptional number of magnificent late 19th-century institutional buildings. In addition, New York City built a series of prominent civic structures, including schools, firehouses, and police stations. As residential development increased, 125th Street became the community's central commercial thoroughfare, with both small shops and larger department stores.

The building boom that created some of Harlem's finest rowhouse blocks lasted until 1893, when a nationwide economic depression not only brought a halt to new investment and construction, but also stagnated rowhouse sales. So serious was this depression that lenders foreclosed on many properties. David H. King, for example, was only able to sell nine of his King Model Houses prior to the economic downturn and in 1895 he was forced to cede the remaining 140 buildings to the mortgagor.

As the economy stabilized in 1895, and as investors reentered the market, Harlem again became the venue for extensive building. Rowhouse development continued in some areas, notably near Hamilton Grange and in the vicinity of the Morris-Jumel Mansion, but most builders turned to the construction of apartment houses. A few of the new buildings were impressively designed structures with expansive apartments, most notably the Graham Court (OS2) on Seventh Avenue and 116th Street. Many others were elevator buildings planned with comfortable units for middle-class families. However, most of the new construction took the form of five-story walkup tenements. The tenements in certain sections of Harlem filled up rapidly as many immigrant groups outgrew the Lower East Side and established new ethnic enclaves. Italians settled in large numbers in East Harlem and Eastern European Jews moved onto the streets between Lenox and Lexington avenues from about 100th Street north to about 119th Street. Although New York City's largest African-American community was located

The beginning of subway construction on Lenox Avenue, looking north from 120th Street in 1901.

in the west Midtown area, Harlem already had enclaves with substantial numbers of black residents.

The beginning of construction on the IRT subway in 1900, with a route along Lenox Avenue in Central Harlem, and another route along Broadway on the Heights, led to what one real estate report called "a violent speculation on unimproved property...and an enormous increase in the construction of tenement houses." In Harlem, the vast majority of these new tenements were sited north of 135th Street in what had once been marshlands. Between 1901 and 1907, over 450 tenements were erected between 135th and 155th streets in Central Harlem. Unfortunately for developers and property owners, the arrival of the subway in 1904 did not have the desired affect on apartment rentals. By the early 20th century, as mass transit facilities out of Manhattan improved, many of Harlem's middle-class residents moved to other boroughs or to the suburbs. In addition, while the subway certainly made Harlem more convenient for those commuting to jobs downtown, it also opened up vast new territories in Washington Heights and in the Bronx where new and often better or less expensive housing competed with the tenements of Harlem.

It was the overbuilding of tenements in the area north of 135th Street, resulting in the inability of owners to find tenants among the white ethnic groups who had previously inhabited most of Harlem's multiple dwellings, that led a few landlords to begin renting to black families. From this initial opening in what had been a restricted housing market, thousands of African-Americans moved to Harlem, seeking apartments in the new tenements that were far superior to accommodations downtown. So rapid was the migration that the black population of Harlem was estimated at about 50,000 by 1914, with the new migrants residing on an increasingly large number of blocks. By the late 1920s, the black population was expanding south of 125th Street into the fine rowhouse blocks of the Mount Morris area.

Very little private development occurred in Central Harlem after the early 20th century. Most of the land had already been built upon and the discriminatory policies of most banks resulted in the rejection of mortgages for new construction in a black neighborhood. Residential construction, however, continued on the Heights, an area that remained unaffected by the changing population in Central Harlem. In the second and third decades of the 20th century, many middle-class elevator buildings of six or more stories were erected with apartments rented to an ethnically mixed group of white tenants. It was not until the 1930s that middle-class African-American families migrated up onto the Heights, purchasing rowhouses and renting in such prominent apartment houses as 409 and 555 Edgecombe Avenue (HH31 and JT11), in the area that came to be known as Sugar Hill.

Since the 1930s, most construction in Harlem has been government sponsored, including large city housing projects, notably the pioneering Harlem River Houses (OS14) of 1936-37. Fortunately, a substantial

The inauguration of
Harlem River Houses,
1937.

amount of Harlem's historic architecture remains. Some
of the older buildings, especially the tenements, have
seriously deteriorated, but many of the rowhouses of
Harlem's finest residential neighborhoods are lovingly
cared for and are attracting a new generation of residents
interested in preserving the architecture and history of
the community.

The Capital of Black America

Gretchen S. Sorin

There are certain places where circumstances, people, and ideas meet to create a momentous historic site. Harlem, as it has evolved into one of America's leading African-American communities, is such a place. While some people think of this neighborhood in upper Manhattan as simply a black ghetto, this false characterization disguises a rich and complex history of struggle and celebration, of success and failure, of hope and dignity. Throughout its history, Harlem has been a place for American dreams. At the beginning of the 20th century it was a place where African-Americans hoped to establish a color-blind community in a color-conscious world. In the 1920s, it was home to poets, writers, and musicians from around the country. In the 1960s it was charged with the excitement and commitment of the Civil Rights Movement. Today, the history of Harlem as an African-American community can still be seen as one walks the streets of the neighborhood: The great churches that have anchored New York's black community; the fine apartment houses and rowhouses where generations of African-Americans have lived; the clubs where black entertainers starred and in which black and white patrons came together to enjoy a show. Harlem is a fascinating historic community, one that is ingrained in our collective past and remains a vital part of New York City.

Among the earliest residents of the colony of New York were black slaves brought by Dutch settlers, including those who settled in Nieuw Haarlem. From the establishment of New York's first free black community in the Wall Street area in the 18th century, the gradual movement northward began. Early black communities in New York City were by nature rather fluid, often being displaced by floods of immigrants, by discrimination enforced by law and by custom, and by the growth of the business district. The Wall Street neighborhood disappeared and was replaced by a community in the Five

Harlem street scene, c.1910-15. The sign reads "Apartments to Let 3 and 4 Rooms with Improvements For Respectable Colored Families Only."

Points slum where black people and poor Irish immigrants lived side by side. By the Civil War era, a large number of Manhattan's African-Americans lived in Greenwich Village, in a settlement centering around tiny Gay Street. By 1900, most of the black community of about 60,000 people had moved into the over-crowded tenements in the Tenderloin, the district west of Seventh Avenue above 23rd Street, or in San Juan Hill in the West 50s. The beginning of construction on Pennsylvania Station in 1904 on two full blocks in the heart of the Tenderloin displaced a large part of the community. These families and new migrants arriving from the South needed places to live, while others were seeking improved housing outside of the Midtown slums. The place many settled was Harlem.

In the early 20th century, with the promise of a new subway line running along Lenox Avenue, property in Harlem changed hands rapidly and hundreds of tenements were erected by small developers who hoped that their investments would appreciate overnight. Unfortunately for these investors, the housing market collapsed. African-American realtor and entrepreneur Philip A. Payton, Jr. saw this as an opportunity. The college-educated Payton developed an interest in real estate while working as a janitor in a real estate office. Payton established the Afro-American Realty Company with ten investors and set about convincing white property owners that their problems finding renters could be solved by opening their buildings to African-Americans. Black families were so anxious for decent housing that they would pay premium rents. Rents in Harlem for African-Americans were considerably higher than those for white residents. Some owners actually preferred crossing the color-line rather than renting to those they referred to as "lower grades of foreign white people."

Payton found his first opportunity to integrate Harlem housing and reap handsome profits by stepping into a dispute between two landlords. One of them asked Payton to manage his building on West 134th Street. This marks the beginning of Harlem as a place in which black people were permitted to live. Gradually, more and more struggling apartment house owners decided to rent to African-Americans or even sold their properties to black investors.

Not everyone in Harlem was happy about the influx of African-Americans. Many property owners refused to rent to black people. They hastily banded together in such organizations as the Anglo-Saxon Realty Corporation and the Harlem Property Owners' Improvement Corporation in an effort to keep African-Americans out of "their" neighborhood. Despite the harsh and racist rhetoric of the publicity campaigns created by some property owners, the desire of others to reap profits and decrease vacancies meant that Harlem was destined to become a black neighborhood. Once some buildings opened to African-American renters, fear that property values would plummet convinced other white owners to sell. Payton had originally entertained the notion that African-American and white tenants could live in the same buildings, but in an age of separate and unequal accommodations, most white people would not accept the notion and the idea of racially integrated buildings was soon abandoned. Segregation in housing, like segregation in theaters, hotels, and most schools was the custom among most Americans, even in the North. With the arrival of blacks in Harlem, white flight began.

The trickle of black migrants to northern cities became a torrent during and after World War I. This Great Migration from the South to the North became the most significant historical event in African-American history after emancipation. Large numbers of southern black people, disgusted with Jim Crow laws and the Ku Klux Klan, fleeing poverty, discrimination, and a lack of opportunity, sought new lives and good jobs. In the ten years between 1910 and 1920, the black population of Manhattan jumped more than 80 percent. There was another substantial jump in population during the next decade. Most of these new residents settled in Harlem which become the unofficial capital of black America. The vibrant new community fostered intense pride and self-determination and encouraged political activism. As the black population grew, the boundaries of black

Harlem expanded until by the 1930s much of Central Harlem was inhabited by African-Americans and prosperous black households were moving west onto the heights overlooking the Harlem Plain. Black businesses also expanded; New York State's largest African-American newspaper, the New York Age, noted that by 1921 about 80% of the businesses near 135th Street and Seventh Avenue were black owned.

Although most of the migrants to Harlem came from the American South, a large number of immigrants from British, Dutch, and French colonies in the West Indies added to the diversity of black Harlem. By the 1930s more than 20% of Harlem's black residents were from the Caribbean. Like their southern brethren, they sought better living conditions for themselves and their families. Cultural differences often created friction between West Indian blacks and African-Americans. Their accents, business acumen, and formal manner, characteristic of

Street Life on Lenox Avenue looking north from West 132nd Street, c. 1928.

*Grocery Store,
Harlem, 1940. Photo
by Aaron Siskind.*

the European influence in their homelands, were inter-
preted as superior behaviors by some. Although they
were not united as a group, West Indians formed support organizations that catered to specific nationalities,
causing some native-born African-Americans to see them
as cliquish. Many West Indians were better educated
than their American neighbors and by the 1930s quite a
high percentage of black businessmen and professionals

were from this region. Religious differences also exacerbated the divisions. West Indians were more likely to be Roman Catholic or Episcopalian than the majority of American born black people who were usually Baptist or Methodist.

Energized within the environment of this new all-black community, the "New Negro" emerged. The "New Negro" had a sense of pride in African-American identity and was angry about being treated as a second-class citizen. The movement was fueled by the Great Migration, which was, in essence, a massive protest against the lack of opportunity in the South and a reflection of the expanded world view of black soldiers returning from World War I. After fighting totalitarianism abroad, black soldiers were angry that their own country was still unwilling to accept them. Jobs and educational opportunities open to white soldiers were unavailable to black soldiers. Some returning heroes were murdered during protests. Within this heightened political environment intellectuals like sociologist W.E.B. DuBois and visionaries like philosopher Alain Locke and Charles Jones, editor of the magazine *Opportunity*, saw artistic achievement as a weapon which could help to break down the barriers between the races. Literature, art, and music which flowed from the folk spirit of African-American communities and contributed positively to American life, they reasoned, would counter such stereotyping as D.W. Griffith's racist film *Birth of a Nation* and the resurgence of the Ku Klux Klan. The poetry of Langston Hughes (OS10) and Claude McKay and the rich stories of African-American life and love by Zora Neale Hurston reflected the diversity, humanity, self assurance, and pride of the "New Negro." Actors, musicians, and visual artists were also drawn to Harlem, often incorporating African-American folk tales and heritage into visual representations of American life. This Harlem Renaissance dawned in 1919 and flourished until 1929.

The excitement of life in Harlem attracted not only African-Americans but also enticed many white Americans uptown for an evening's entertainment or to purchase a work of art. Some were genuinely interested in

Fletcher Henderson
and His Band, 1936.

an America that was not race conscious. Others were
lured by what they saw as the exoticism of black people.
The night clubs of Harlem nourished both desires. The
Apollo (OS5) and Lafayette theaters offered integrated
audiences stage shows and the new jazz music along
with ragtime and blues. Harlem nightlife included performances by James Reese Europe (one of the most popular band and dance leaders in the country prior to
World War I), Duke Ellington (OS14), Ethel Waters,
Fletcher Henderson (HC22), Florence Mills (HC12), Cab
Calloway, Bessie Smith, Ella Fitzgerald, and innumerable
chorus girls. Many of the popular dances of the jazz age
originated here—the Turkey Trot, the Black Bottom, and
Ballin' the Jack. In Harlem clubs such as Small's Paradise
(HC8) and the Renaissance Casino (HC20) people, both
black and white, interacted, ate, drank and got to know
one another in the spirit of integration. It was the America that many hoped for. But even in Harlem's golden
age, there was racial prejudice. The famous Cotton Club,
for example, was restricted. The club hired African-
American entertainers to play to an all white, segregated
house. The music of W.C. Handy (HC22) was frequently
played here, but Handy was turned away at the door.

In addition to arts and culture, the activism of the
"New Negro" was reflected in the diversity of political

institutions and an abundance of political activity. The corner of 125th Street and Lenox Avenue was so often the scene of a public political lecture, march, or discussion that it was dubbed "The Street Corner University." The myriad political institutions provided ample room for different opinions and multiple solutions to the problems of the color line. The corner of 135th Street and Seventh Avenue was a political nerve center in Harlem. Many political-party organizations, unions, and civil rights groups were headquartered near this intersection, including the Harlem branch of the Urban League (HC16), Marcus Garvey's United Negro Improvement Organization (HC15), and the Brotherhood of Sleeping Car Porters (HC17).

Harlem churches were among the most influential and politically powerful institutions in the community. These centers of spiritual leadership were, as black churches have traditionally been in the United States, also forces in politics, social welfare, and community development. They provided a forum in which black leaders could learn and practice leadership skills and the nucleus of a large membership whose numbers could be called upon at a moment's notice. New York City's most

St. Nicholas Presbyterian Church in 1926, one year before it was transferred to St. James, a black Presbyterian congregation. In the forground, construction is proceeding on the IND subway.

25

historic African-American churches, including St. Philip's Episcopal (HC10), Mother A.M.E. Zion (HC32), St. Mark's Methodist (HC26), St. James Presbyterian (HH6), and Adam Clayton Powell, Sr.'s Abyssinian Baptist (HC30) abandoned their Midtown locations following their congregations to Harlem. Some congregations erected new buildings (a few commissioning designs from black architects), but others purchased the churches and synagogues of white congregations whose memberships were dwindling as worshippers left the neighborhood. Many new congregations were established to cater to the spiritual needs of the expanding population. As southern African-Americans moved in, storefront churches were founded, drawing worshippers from those unfamiliar with the staid practices of the major Protestant faiths and those desiring a more exuberant form of worship.

The seemingly limitless opportunities of an all-black community and the glitz and excitement of Harlem's night life and growing artistic community hid the fact that Harlem was fast becoming a slum. The tremendous demand for housing caused by the massive number of incoming residents drove the already premium rents higher. Since African-American's wages were lower than the national average, people struggled simply to make ends meet. Often, they could not. Rent parties were held to raise money to pay the landlord. Landlords often converted apartment houses and single-family rowhouses into single-room-occupancy tenements, filling their buildings beyond capacity. Maintenance on many buildings declined precipitously. Crime, disease, and overcrowding were rampant. The onset of the Great Depression in 1929 made conditions even worse. Widespread unemployment, inflated food and rent costs, and frustration over continuing racism in the United States erupted into a riot in 1935. A second riot in 1943 illustrated the ongoing tensions and economic privation within the community.

Many Harlem residents became involved in direct, non-violent action within the community to change the deplorable conditions. The "Don't Buy Where You Can't

Work" campaign of the 1930s is an example of positive action, resulting in the employment of black workers as clerks in local stores like Blumstein's (OS7), Harlem's largest department store. However, such triumphs alone were not enough to stem the tide of urban poverty and joblessness.

World War II, like the first World War brought a concerted effort by African-Americans to address urban problems and American racism at home as many had

Adam Clayton Powell, Jr., Jacqueline Kennedy, John F. Kennedy, and Eleanor Roosevelt campaigning on 125th Street in front of the Hotel Theresa in 1960.

fought and died to end it abroad. While defense factories improved the economies of some states, New York had few defense industries and the black community in Harlem recovered extremely slowly from the Great Depression. Poverty, unemployment, and violence became an ever-present part of life. In the midst of this, African-Americans developed strategies that would become the hallmark of the non-violent Civil Rights Movement of the 1950s and 1960s. Marches and protests signaled the start of a massive push for equality, voting rights, and an end to segregation. Organizations like the NAACP, CORE (The Congress of Racial Equality), and local churches nurtured leaders. Most notable was the Reverend Adam Clayton Powell, Jr. of the Abyssinian Baptist Church who became Harlem's first African-American congressman in 1944. These groups also provided support for the large numbers of northerners who went South on freedom marches. Harlem became one of

Malcolm X speaking at
Marcus Garvey Day
celebration in 1958.

many staging grounds for the Movement. The leader of
the Civil Rights Movement, Dr. Martin Luther King, Jr.,
came here to speak and to rally supporters.

The slow pace of racial progress and the intractable

nature of poverty and racism led some African-Americans to adopt a rhetoric that offered a new approach to race problems in the United States to black Americans, but appeared angry to white Americans. The leader of this new form of black nationalism was Malcolm X who became one of the most outspoken African-American leaders during the 1960s and often held rallies on Lenox Avenue which were attended by hundreds of people hungry for an improvement in their lives. In 1964, Malcolm X broke his ties with the Nation of Islam and founded his own organization in New York, the Organization of Afro-American Unity, with offices in the Hotel Theresa (OS6). He had little opportunity to put his new ideas into practice before his assassination at the Audubon Ballroom in nearby Washington Heights in February, 1965.

The Civil Rights Movement of the 1960s brought some unexpected changes to Harlem's circumstances. As some previously segregated communities opened to African-Americans, much of Harlem's middle class left, leaving a large concentration of poor people. For the African-American migrants arriving last in American cities, the opportunities available were more limited than for those European immigrants arriving before the cities began to decline. Grass roots organizations and churches worked to improve living conditions, bring more businesses to Harlem, and preserve or in many cases rebuild neighborhoods. These organizations also remained active in the ongoing national struggle for civil rights.

Hope springs forth in Harlem today as it did during the early years of this century. Although the community still struggles, along the broad avenues are thriving businesses and here and there along tree-lined side streets are old buildings being rescued. The buildings of Harlem are representative of an important part of the history of New York City, the history of black America, and of our collective past as Americans. These buildings, monuments to all that Harlem has been and will be, rekindle our links with the culture and history of this historic American place and the dreams that flourished here long ago and that flourish here still.

A Note on the Tours

Today, the large area of northern Manhattan named Harlem by the Dutch is divided into several separate neighborhoods, each with its own identity. These include Central Harlem (generally referred to simply as Harlem), East Harlem (also known as Spanish Harlem), Hamilton Heights (sometimes called West Harlem or Sugar Hill), and Washington Heights. The tours in this book encompass blocks in several of these areas.

The guide consists of four walking tours, each centering on a historic district designated by the New York City Landmarks Preservation Commission, but including buildings outside the district boundaries. The entries include those concerned primarily with the architecture and early development of Harlem and those of significance to the African-American history of the community. We hope that these will provide both those pounding the pavement and those reading in an armchair at home with a well-rounded introduction to the architecture and development of some of Harlem's finest sections and the transformation of Harlem into one of America's great centers of African-American life.

Each tour is written as a complete unit. Tours vary considerably in length. The Jumel Terrace tour, for example, is quite short, but the architectural and cultural history of the area between West 135th and 139th streets, referred to here as Harlem Central, is so rich and varied that this tour is quite long. There is no reason why longer tours cannot be split into sections that are walked separately. There are so many fascinating buildings in Harlem that it is impossible to include all of them on walking tours of reasonable length. We apologize if your favorite building has been excluded or if a place of great historic interest does not appear. We have added a section that includes a selection of additional sites in Harlem located outside of the tours in the hope that this will assist in further exploration within the neighborhood.

While taking the tours there are a few things you should keep in mind. When looking at a building, you may find that you can see more if you stand on the opposite side of the street where a comprehensive view of a structure and its setting can be had. You may wish, however, to get up close to a building to examine details. Most buildings are named for their original owner or use. In the case of buildings associated with people or organizations of historic interest, the name chosen generally relates to this. Current building names are provided where applicable. The indices should aid in finding a particular structure or historic site. Those not familiar with Harlem should remember that Lenox Avenue (also known as Malcolm X Boulevard) is the equivalent of Sixth Avenue, Adam Clayton Powell, Jr. Boulevard is Seventh Avenue, and Frederick Douglass Boulevard is Eighth Avenue. Remember that most of the buildings on the tour are private and are not open to the public.

A Note on the Photographs

In addition to the text discussing the architecturally and historically important sites, we have included a large number of photographs in this guide book. We have chosen only historic views of Harlem so that those walking the tours can compare early views with the contemporary scene. In addition, for those reading at home, the photographs will complement the text. We were fortunate in being able to acquire the rights to photographs taken by several prominent African-American photographers. Beginning in the 1920s, a group of black photographers, including Austin Hansen, Aaron Siskind, and James Van Der Zee became active in Harlem, photographing local streets, African-American celebrities, religious and fraternal groups, famous entertainment spots, and average citizens going about their daily lives. These photographs create an incomparable record of life in Harlem.

West 121st Street and Lenox Avenue with Mount Morris Park in background, summer 1883.

Mount Morris Tour

Introduction

The area to the west of Mount Morris Park, centering on Lenox Avenue between West 118th and 124th streets, was one of the first in Harlem to attract residential development following the opening of the elevated railroads. The neighborhood was ideally suited for new development since it was close to the rail lines on Eighth and Third avenues, but not so close that the blocks were marred by the noise and dirt of the trains. In the early 1880s a number of brownstone-fronted rows appeared on Mount Morris Park West and adjacent streets. Major development, however, did not begin until 1885 and by the end of the decade several hundred homes had appeared. The rowhouses were primarily occupied by prosperous white Protestant households, with workers commuting to jobs downtown. By the turn of the century, many of the original residents were moving out and less wealthy people, both native born and immigrant, moved in. Many of the single-family rowhouses were converted into rooming houses. Among the new residents were large numbers of Eastern European Jewish immigrants who settled in the southeastern part of the Mount Morris area, at the edge of New York City's second largest Jewish immigrant neighborhood (after the Lower East Side). In the late 1920s black households began moving into the area. Prosperous African-American owners maintained some of the houses as single-family dwellings, but many others continued as rooming houses or were divided into apartments. The complex nature of population succession in the Mount Morris area is echoed in the history of its magnificent religious structures. Today, the neighborhood has an increasingly large number of owner-occupied, single-family dwellings, as more and more people have discovered the beauty of Mount Morris rowhouses and have purchased and restored the homes.

The New York City Landmarks Preservation Commission designated the Mount Morris Park Historic District in 1971, but the boundaries were limited to buildings along Lenox Avenue and the streets between Lenox and Mount Morris Park (renamed Marcus Garvey Park in 1973). An intensive effort on the part of the Mount Morris Community Association in recent years aided by the New York Landmarks Conservancy, has resulted in the listing of a larger area on the National Register of Historic Places and a proposal to extend the city landmark district westward towards Adam Clayton Powell, Jr. Boulevard.

Tour

MM1 Lenox Avenue

Start: Northwest corner Lenox Avenue and West 123rd Street. From this corner you can see the first four entries.

Lenox Avenue, the northern extension of Sixth Avenue, was named in 1887 in honor of one of the city's wealthiest and most prominent families; the street has been renamed for another of the city's most significant figures, Malcolm X. This is one of the widest avenues in New York City and, according to a description in 1889, was "lined with grass plots and handsome trees at both sides, and these, when in leaf, enhance the appearance of the houses." The houses are on a grand scale, most four full stories above a high basement. This is evident on the western blockfront between 122nd and 123rd streets where the brownstone-fronted dwellings are some of the earliest erected on the avenue (No. 241, A.B. Van Dusen, 1883-85; Nos. 243-259 Charles H. Beer, 1885-86). During the 20th century, Lenox Avenue became a central thoroughfare of black Harlem. On this street protest marchers walked, political speakers preached on soap boxes, and fashionable men, women, and children strolled. Some of Harlem's most prominent businesses, night clubs, and community organizations were clustered on or near this avenue.

MM2 Reformed Low Dutch Church of Harlem (Second Reformed Church of Harlem)

Now Ephesus Seventh Day Adventist Church, 267 Lenox Avenue, northwest corner West 123rd Street (John R.

The *Ephesus Seventh Day Adventist* Church in 1932.

Thomas, church and rectory, 1885-87; church hall at rear, 1894-95). The rowhouses on Lenox Avenue rose beside impressive institutional buildings such as this Gothic-inspired structure faced in yellowish Ohio sandstone. Prominent architect John Rochester Thomas (best known for his Hall of Records/Surrogate's Court on Chambers Street) designed a church with a slender tapering tower that was once capped by a metal crocket. A close examination of the lower level will reveal fine carved capitals and such details as corbels in the form of monsters flanking the central entrance and the mustachioed head of a man set between the doors. In 1930, as the white Protestant population in the area ebbed, the church was leased to the Ephesus Seventh Day Adventist congregation which purchased the building in 1939. Ephesus was established through a merger of New York's two oldest black Adventist congregations. Sadly, the original interior was destroyed in a fire in 1969. In 1968, the Boys Choir of Harlem was founded here as an effort to help children realize their potential and achieve success in all areas of their lives.

James Van Der Zee's G.G.G. Studio at 272 Lenox Avenue in 1945. Photo by James Van Der Zee.

MM3 James Van Der Zee Studio

272 Lenox Avenue (Charles H. Beer, 1885-86). The G.G.G. Photo Studio of the great photographer James Van Der Zee (1886-1983) was located in the ground floor of this rowhouse (the second house from the left) from 1942 until 1969. Here, and in his earlier studios (HC4), he captured Harlem images on film as Langston Hughes had captured them in poetry. His formal portraits of artists, great leaders, and ordinary African-Americans, his street scenes, and his photographs of church groups, funerals, weddings, and fraternal organizations reflect the intense confidence and pride that African-Americans in Harlem felt about their community and their future. Recognized as one of the most significant American photographers and a major contributor to the Harlem Renaissance, Van Der Zee was also a historian, providing one of the largest photographic records of Harlem during the first half of the 20th century. Van Der Zee photographs can be seen on pages 80 and 86.

Harlem Club, c. 1888.

MM4 Harlem Club

Now Bethelite Community Church, 34 West 123rd
Street, southeast corner Lenox Avenue (Lamb & Rich,
1888-89). The Harlem Club was the leading social organization for the affluent Protestant families who purchased many of Harlem's new rowhouses. The building
is one of the most spectacular Queen Anne structures in
the city. Its lively facade is faced with red-hued brick,
stone, and terra cotta in varied textures. The roofline of
the Lenox Avenue frontage is especially fine with its central gable flanked by tall chimneys, and two spectacular
hooded dormers clad in Spanish tile. The interior originally contained dining rooms, a library, billiard and card
rooms, and bowling alleys. The club did not occupy the
building long. Dissension among members coupled with
changes in the population of the neighborhood led to a
bank foreclosure in 1907. The building has been a
church since 1947.

Cross Lenox
Avenue and walk
east on West
123rd Street.

MM5 Harlem Library

Now Greater Bethel A.M.E. Church, 32 West 123rd
Street (Edgar K. Bourne, 1891-92). The Harlem Library,

Harlem Library, 1892.

with roots dating back to 1820, was one of the first publicly accessible libraries in New York City. This small, picturesque limestone and brick building, designed by a member of the library's board of trustees, was erected to serve Harlem's rapidly growing population. In 1901, the library became a part of the New York Public Library system and in 1909 the collection moved into a larger building still in use at 9-11 West 124th Street (McKim, Mead & White, 1907-09). The present owner, Greater Bethel A.M.E. Church, is one of the oldest black churches in New York, founded in Lower Manhattan in 1819. By 1840, Bethel had opened a mission that catered to Harlem's small black community. The main church finally settled in Harlem in the early 20th century.

MM6 28-30 West 123rd Street

(John E. Terhune, 1884-85). This fanciful pair of exceptionally narrow houses, each only thirteen feet wide, contrasts dramatically with the more traditional brownstone rowhouses to the east (MM7). The Queen Anne pair illustrates a new freedom in design as architects in the 1880s broke away from the box-like form of rowhouses faced with smooth brownstone. Instead, brick and stone in varied colors and textures was combined with oddly-scaled window panes, an interesting rooftop silhouette, and exuberant ornament. The tall slender flower that grows from an urn carved between the doors, the floral panels below the parlor-floor windows, and the chrysanthemums that ornament the original wooden doors are among the many especially fine features.

MM7 4-26 West 123rd Street

(Charles Baxter, 1880-1882). Most of the early rowhouses in the Mount Morris area are high-stooped, brownstone-fronted dwellings designed in the Neo-Grec style, a mode of design identifiable by the use of simple incised ornament and angular detail (notably the brackets of the rooftop cornices). Brownstone, a type of sandstone, was first used for rowhouse facades in the 1840s and became so popular that today New Yorkers refer to all rowhouses as "brownstones," irrespective of their actual facade material. Much of the brownstone was quarried in Connecticut and shipped down the Connecticut River to stone yards in the city. By the 1880s, when these houses were erected, the fashion for brownstone was on the wane as distant quarries and factories sent stones and bricks of varied colors to the city on the expanding railroad network.

Continue walking east towards the corner of Mount Morris Park West.

40

MM8 John and Nancy Dwight Residence

Now Commandment Keepers Ethiopian Hebrew Congregation, 31 Mount Morris Park West, northwest corner West 123rd Street (Frank H. Smith, 1889-90). This mansion was commissioned by baking soda magnate John Dwight whose "Arm and Hammer" brand remains a best-seller. It is an Italian Renaissance-inspired structure with an especially handsome entrance enframement. After serving as a sanitarium for many years, the house was converted into a synagogue in 1962. During the early 20th century, several congregations of black Jews were organized in Harlem. Many of these adherents to Judaism were West Indians who viewed people of African descent as one of the lost tribes of Israel. The largest and best known of these congregations was the building's present occupant, the Commandment Keepers Congregation. It was organized in 1930 by Rabbi W.A. Matthew, a Nigerian who emigrated first to St. Kitts in the West Indies and then to the United States and who graduated from the Jewish Theological Seminary.

Doorway of the Dwight Residence, 1890.

MM9 26-30 Mount Morris Park West

(A.B. Van Dusen, 1880-81). Note, on this impressive row of brownstone, Neo-Grec houses, the stylized incised floral carving, the high stoops with heavy stone newel posts, and the elegant entrance porticos. Soon after its completion, No. 26 became the home of notorious Tammany political boss Richard Crocker.

Turn right onto Mount Morris Park West.

Walk to the corner of West 122nd Street.

MM10 Harlem Presbyterian Church

Later Harlem-New York Presbyterian Church/later Mount Morris Presbyterian Church/now Mount Morris Ascension Presbyterian Church, 16-20 Mount Morris Park West, southwest corner West 122nd Street (Thomas H. Poole, 1905-06). Unquestionably one of the oddest church buildings in New York, this structure is clad in rough granite with vertical bands of gold Roman brick. The squared-off roofline hides a tall dome that is only fully visible from a distance. The Harlem Presbyterian Church, with a history dating back to 1844, erected the church independently. It merged in 1915 with the New

York Presbyterian Church which moved as a result of the increase in the African-American population in the neighborhood surrounding its church on Seventh Avenue and West 128th Street. The united congregation left the Mount Morris area in 1942 for the same reason, merging with the Rutgers Presbyterian Church on West 73rd Street. The Presbytery of New York took over the vacant church, presenting it to a black Presbyterian congregation that has thrived at this location.

Turn right and walk part way down West 122nd Street.

8-12 West 122nd Street in c.1940.

MM11 4-16 West 122nd Street

(William B. Tuthill, 1888-89). William Tuthill was a little-known architect who, two years after the completion of this row, inexplicably received the commission for Carnegie Hall. These conservative brownstone-fronted houses with their Renaissance-inspired carved detail and extensive series of stained-glass transoms, are anchored

by a series of extraordinary stone stoops. The high stoop is a distinguishing element of the New York City rowhouse. Most houses have simple straight stoops, but here several of the boldly-scaled stoops have multiple turns and massive newel posts. Even more dynamic stoops sweep up to the front doors of Nos. 13-15 (Cleverdon & Putzel, 1887-88) across the street. Occupancy in the rowhouses on 122nd Street has remained quite stable. As late as 1925, when most houses in the area had been subdivided, many of these remained single-family dwellings, as most are today.

11-14 Mount Morris Park West and 1 West 121st Street in c. 1889.

Return to Mount Morris Park West and turn right. Walk towards 121st Street.

MM12 11-14 Mount Morris Park West and 1 West 121st Street

(James E. Ware, 1887-89). These five picturesque brick houses, with their French-inspired gables and corner tower (once capped by a conical roof), were sold to families that were typical of those in the Mount Morris area. Most early owners were American-born business or professional men who lived here with their wives (none employed outside of the house) and children. Each household had at least one and often two servants, mostly young immigrant women. These women used service as a way of getting established in America. Few stayed at the same household for long, marrying or seeking factory work in order to get out of service, or moving to a new household in order to acquire better wages or a less onerous position. Servants received minimal pay, had little privacy, and often toiled without interruption and with few modern conveniences for fourteen hours and were then on call for the rest of the day. By the 1920s, these and many nearby dwellings had become rooming houses with large numbers of Eastern European Jewish inhabitants. It was not until about 1930 that black households began to move into the houses adjoining Mount Morris Park.

Walk to the corner of West 121st Street.

Mount Morris Park fire watch tower in the late 19th century.

MM13 Mount Morris Park Watch Tower

Marcus Garvey Park (Julius B. Kroehl, 1855). Land for Mount Morris Park was acquired by the city in 1839; a new park welcomed Harlem's small population three years later. In 1973, the park was renamed for black nationalist Marcus Garvey (HC15). At the crest of the 70' high rocky outcropping in the center of the park stands New York's only surviving cast-iron fire watch tower (depending upon the leaf cover, it is visible, at least in part, from this corner). It is an octagonal structure with Doric columns supporting a platform and small covered observatory. A spiral stair ascends to the observatory and the bell that was rung to announce a fire hangs from bowed iron girders. With the installation of fire alarm boxes in about 1870, fire towers became obsolete and most were demolished. Although sadly deteriorated and awaiting a planned restoration, the Mount Morris tower is an extraordinary survivor from the period when Harlem was largely a rural and suburban community.

6-10 Mount Morris
Park West in 1892.

MM14a 1-5 Mount Morris Park West

(Gilbert A. Schellenger, 1893) and **MM14b 6-10
Mount Morris Park West** (Edward L. Angell, 1891).
There are few sadder sites in Harlem then this blockfront
of once-elegant rowhouses, several of which have com-
pletely lost their facades. The two rows of single-family
homes once stretched along the entire blockfront. In
1923-24 a sanitarium replaced the corner house (Henry
A. Koelble, architect); this building is now a women's
prison. The remaining rowhouses deteriorated after New
York State took the property by eminent domain in 1968
with plans to create a drug rehabilitation center. This
proposal was stopped by community opposition as was a
more recent plan to expand the prison. The future of this
site remains uncertain.

MM15 4-22 and 13-21 West 121st Street

(Cleverdon & Putzel, 1887-90). The firm of Cleverdon &
Putzel was the most prolific designer in the Mount Morris area. Robert Cleverdon and Joseph Putzel typify the
architects of speculatively built rowhouses. Although
responsible for hundreds of rowhouses in Harlem and
on the Upper East and West sides, little is known about
their lives. They probably had little formal training and

Turn right onto
West 121st Street.

exemplify the type of designer whom the influential turn-of-the-century architectural critic Montgomery Schuyler refused to recognize as architects, but instead denigrated as merely "the speculative builder's draughts-men." Cleverdon & Putzel and their compatriots did, however, provide middle-class households with fashionable dwellings that could, when the economy and related market forces cooperated, provide substantial profits to the builders. Many of the houses on the north side have the whimsical carved decoration often provided by the speculative builders.

Walk to Lenox Avenue. Note the vista west towards the tower of Riverside Church.

MM16   Lenox Avenue Unitarian Church

Later Congregation and Chebra Ukadisha B'nai Israel Mikalwarie/Now Ebenezer Gospel Tabernacle, 225 Lenox Avenue, northwest corner West 121st Street (Charles Atwood, 1889-91). The history of this lovely little Gothic Revival church building illustrates the changing character of Harlem's population. At the time of its construction, this was the third Unitarian church in New York City and the only one located north of 34th Street. The congregation was drawn from the Protestant families resident in nearby rowhouses. In 1919, by which time there were probably few Unitarians remaining in the neighborhood, the building was sold to a congregation of largely poor Orthodox Jewish immigrants from Eastern Europe (a star of David is still visible in the stained glass on the second story of the gable on 121st Street). Members probably lived in nearby tenements and rooming houses. In 1942, the building was sold to an African-American church congregation, reflecting the fact that most nearby residents were now black.

Cross Lenox Avenue and turn left. Walk towards West 120th Street.

MM17   Temple Israel of Harlem

Now Mount Olivet Baptist Church, 201-203 Lenox Avenue, northwest corner West 120th Street (Arnold W. Brunner, 1906-07). Temple Israel, which became one of Harlem's most prestigious Jewish congregations, was organized in 1870. As Harlem's population grew and as more Jews, especially prosperous reformed Jews of German ancestry, settled in the area, the congregation grew

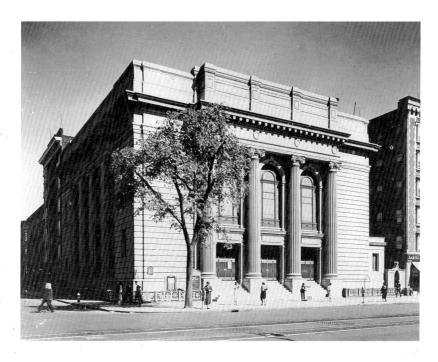

in size and prestige. In 1906, construction began on this impressive limestone structure designed by Arnold Brunner. Brunner, a member of the city's German-Jewish community, was a sophisticated architect who had studied at the Ecole des Beaux-Arts in Paris. He pioneered in the design of grand Classical Revival synagogues, employing as a precedent the Second Temple in Jerusalem which had been built during the Roman period in Palestine and which recent archaeological excavations had shown was in a Roman Classical style. The congregation only occupied the building for thirteen years, for by 1920 most of the synagogue's members had moved out of the neighborhood. This congregation of affluent Jews moved from the neighborhood only a year before the congregation of poor Orthodox Jews purchased the nearby Unitarian church (MM16). The building briefly housed a Seventh Day Adventist church, but in 1925 was purchased by the Mount Olivet Baptist Church which has maintained the building in exceptional condition ever since.

Temple Israel/Mt. Olivet Baptist Church photographed by the Federal Writers Project in 1936.

Return north on Lenox Avenue, walking to the corner of West 121st Street.

MM18a 200-218 Lenox Avenue

Between West 120th and West 121st Streets (deMeuron & Smith, 1887-88) and **MM18b 220-228 Lenox Avenue** Northeast corner West 121st Street (F. Carles Merry, 1888-89). These two rows are indicative of the elegance of Lenox Avenue in the late 19th century. The blockfront between 120th and 121st streets retains much of its original grandeur, despite the loss of one house and several unfortunate alterations. The mansard roof, with its iron cresting, is especially impressive. Between 1894 and 1910, No. 202 was home to famous music publisher Carl Fischer and his family. The boldly-scaled brick and stone houses north of 121st Street retain enormous stoops, rough and smooth stone bases, brick upper stories, and Romanesque- and Renaissance-inspired decorative features. The richness of their exteriors continues inside, where, one commentator noted, "no expense seems to have been spared in the interior embellishments, from the very entrance to the roof." Oak and mahogany woodwork, intricate parquet floors, handsome mantelpieces and built-in buffets, stained-glass windows, and modern plumbing enhanced each dwelling.

Continue north to the corner of West 122nd Street.

MM19 Holy Trinity Episcopal Church

Now St. Martin's Episcopal Church, 230 Lenox Avenue, southeast corner West 122nd Street (William A. Potter, 1887-89). Unquestionably the finest Romanesque Revival style church building surviving in New York City, this boldly-massed structure built of rough red granite with brownstone trim is a masterpiece by one of America's most talented late 19th-century architects. The complex is arranged with the parish house facing Lenox Avenue, the sanctuary to the east, and a rectory on West 122nd Street. The most extraordinary aspect of the design is the sophisticated interpenetration of the simple masses—the tall, pyramidal-roofed open tower (now housing a carillon) and the solid gables of the church house, transept, nave, and rectory. The interior of the church burned in 1926 and the white congregation decided not to rebuild in Harlem, moving instead to

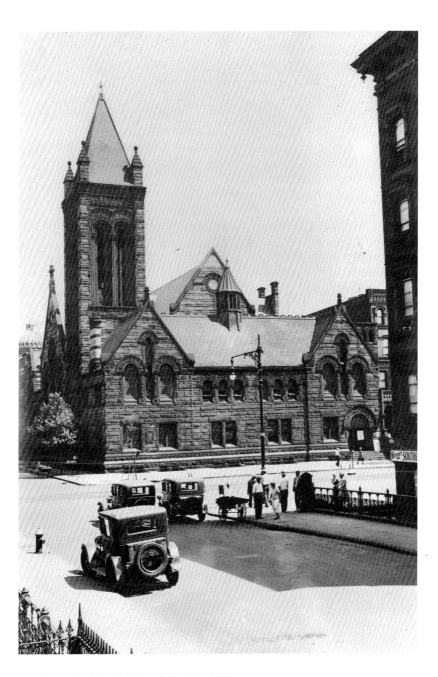

Holy Trinity/St. Martin's Episcopal Church in 1932.

Inwood. St. Martin's acquired the church in 1928 and undertook a restoration. Unfortunately, an even more serious fire in 1939 destroyed all but the massive granite walls. St. Martin's was one of a number of new congregations established by Caribbean immigrants who were more likely to be Episcopalian than were American-born blacks. During the 1930s, the Reverend John Johnson was one of the most influential and politically-active leaders in the black community. Johnson actively supported the "Don't Buy Where You Can't Work" campaign that urged African-American shoppers to boycott businesses that did not hire black employees (OS7).

Turn left on West 122nd Street.

MM20 103-111 West 122nd Street

(Thom & Wilson, 1887-88). Like Cleverdon & Putzel, whose houses line 121st Street (MM15), Thom & Wilson was an extremely prolific designer of speculative rowhouses in the neighborhoods opened to development by the elevated railroads in the late 19th century. These five houses are flamboyantly detailed, with Moorish-inspired horseshoe arches at several of the basement windows; superb carving on the original double doors; and a plethora of carved flowers, fruits, shells, birds, winged griffins, and sea creatures. The more closely you look at the facades, the more wonderful detail you will see.

Continue west on 122nd Street.

MM21 131 West 122nd Street

(Julius Franke, 1890). The influence of Henry Hobson Richardson's architecture is evident on this fine Romanesque Revival house with its round-arched openings; massive stone blocks so roughly textured that they appear to have been ripped out of a quarry (in truth their rough texture was carefully created); and beautiful stained glass. The house is faced in limestone quarried in Indiana and transported to New York by railroad.

MM22 133-143 West 122nd Street

(Francis H. Kimball, 1885-87). This spectacular row of houses, perhaps the finest row of Queen Anne dwellings in New York City, was not designed by an architect who

131 West 122nd
Street in c. 1940.

specialized in speculative construction as were almost all
of the other rowhouses in Harlem. Rather, these five
houses were the work of Francis H. Kimball, one of the
city's leading architects. Kimball's English training is evident on these houses which would not be out of place on
a street in London. Despite the varied textures, the complex projecting and receding planes, and the multiplicity
of gables and dormers at the roofline, the row appears as
a single, elegantly integrated unit. Kimball was one of
the first architects to extensively employ terra cotta for
ornamental detail, as is evident at the decoration above
the parlor floor. Terra cotta is a clay material that was
molded into ornate blocks permitting the creation of
complex decoration at modest cost.

Continue west to
Adam Clayton
Powell, Jr.
Boulevard.

51

MM23 Seventh Avenue

Historically, Seventh Avenue was the busiest thoroughfare of black Harlem. Shops, theaters, clubs, and other
establishments lined the streets and on Sunday after-
noons in the 1920s and 1930s well-dressed Harlemites
paraded their finery down the avenue. Seventh Avenue
also hosted political marches, rallies, and celebrations,
including the celebration of Joe Lewis's heavyweight
boxing victory, and rallies for Marcus Garvey and Malcolm X. Seventh Avenue has been renamed in honor of
Adam Clayton Powell, Jr., Harlem's first black congressman.

MM24 Washington Apartments

2034-2040 Adam Clayton Powell, Jr. Boulevard, southwest corner West 122nd Street (Mortimer C. Merritt,
1883-84). Designed in the fashionable Queen Anne style
that was popular with rowhouse architects (MM6 and
MM22), the Washington was the first middle-class apartment building erected in Harlem. The construction of
the Washington illustrates the changing nature of middle-class housing in New York, as multiple dwellings
came to be an acceptable alternative to the rowhouse for
prosperous households. Constructed of red brick, with a
stone base and prominent rooftop pediment, the eight-
story building originally housed thirty households,
including many professionals and businessmen who
commuted to work on the new elevated railroad with its
nearby station at Eighth Avenue and 125th Street.

Harlem Central Tour

Introduction

In 1892, the blocks between Seventh Avenue (now Adam Clayton Powell, Jr. Boulevard) and Eighth Avenue (now Frederick Douglass Boulevard) just north of West 135th Street, the heart of this walking tour, were referred to as "the cream section" of northern Manhattan. After taking this walk, it will be obvious why this term was used, since you will be on some of New York City's most beautiful residential streets. Development in this area did not occur until the late 1880s and 1890s, despite the fact that an elevated railroad station had opened on 135th Street and Eighth Avenue in 1879, with service to Wall Street in only 35 minutes. In the early 1880s, Harlem in the West 130s was simply too far north for speculative developers who were still heavily engaged in construction on the Upper West Side and other neighborhoods farther south. There was, however, a great deal of land speculation in the vicinity, culminating in 1887 and 1888 when the Equitable Life Assurance Society invested approximately $4,000,000 in the purchase of land from 135th to 142nd streets between Seventh and Eighth avenues. In the early 1890s, Equitable sold most of this property to builders who erected long rows of houses. This included the sale of four blockfronts on West 138th and 139th streets to David H. King, Jr. who erected his masterful King Model Houses complex in 1891-93. Besides rowhouses, this tour includes interesting tenements and apartment buildings and several institutional structures erected during the initial period of development and population growth in the neighborhood.

The area north of 135th Street and east of Seventh Avenue was the first in Harlem to receive a large influx of African-American residents. By the 1920s, the area around 135th Street and Seventh Avenue was the center of Harlem's black community. A character in Nella Larson's novel *Quicksand* (1928) noted "that if one stands on

Central Harlem looking east from City College (Main Hall at right) in 1911. The photographic legend is incorrect since this view shows 140th Street, with its elevated station at left. The King Model Houses are visible in the center. Photo by Irving Underhill.

the corner of 135th Street and 7th Avenue long enough, one will eventually see all the people one has ever known or met." Many of the community's important cultural, political, religious, and recreational organizations were located nearby, including many discussed on this tour.

For the most part, this section of Harlem has aged gracefully, with many well-preserved, owner-occupied rowhouses. The New York City Landmarks Preservation Commission designated Striver's Row as the St. Nicholas Historic District in 1967 and several other buildings are individual landmarks, but, as you will see as you walk, there are many more blocks and buildings deserving designation and preservation.

Tour

Start: Northwest corner Lenox Avenue and West 135th Street.

HC1 Schomburg Center for Research in Black Culture, The New York Public Library

515 Lenox Avenue, northwest corner West 135th Street (Bond Ryder Associates, 1969-80). The Schomburg Center contains one of the world's greatest collections dedicated to the study of black culture throughout the world. The collection is named for Arthur A. Schomburg (1874-1938), a bibliophile, historian, writer, and editor whose collection forms the backbone of the center's holdings. Schomburg was born and educated in Puerto Rico, coming to New York in 1891. At a time when the history of black people was not a valued topic of study, Schomburg began amassing photographs, maps, prints, newspapers, and books from around the world documenting their presence and accomplishments. With funds from the Carnegie Corporation, the New York Public Library purchased the collection for its newly formed Division of Negro Literature, History and Prints in 1926. In 1932, Schomburg was named curator of this collection, which was initially housed next door, at the former 135th Street Branch Library (HC3). The collection was officially named for Schomburg two years after his death.

HC2 Pig Foot Mary's

Corner Lenox Avenue and West 135th Street. This corner was the home of a tiny stand operated by one of Harlem's shrewdest entrepreneurs. Her name was Lillian Harris, but she was known in the neighborhood as Pig Foot Mary. Harris peddled boiled pigs feet, first from a shabby old baby buggy, and later, as her business grew, from a steam table in a booth attached to the corner newspaper stand. Harris found a ready market for her foods among migrants from the South and turned a three dollar investment into a successful business. She used her earnings to invest in Harlem real estate, eventually earning several hundred thousand dollars.

Walk west on 135th Street.

HC3 New York Public Library, 135th Street Branch

Now part of Schomburg Center, 103 West 135th Street

(McKim, Mead & White, 1903-05). Following Andrew Carnegie's 1901 gift of $5,000,000 to the New York Public Library, a series of neighborhood libraries was erected. Charles McKim and his assistant William Kendall provided sensitive, superbly detailed designs for 11 of the new branches (HH16). Among the notable features of this building, modelled on a palazzo in Verona, Italy, are the arched Palladian window on the second story with its fine iron screen, the seal of the city set above this window, and the beltcourse between the first and second stories that is appropriately ornamented with open books. During the early 1920s, Ernestine Rose, the branch librarian, compiled a collection of African-American titles and in 1925 the library was renamed the 135th Street Branch Division of Negro Literature. It later housed the Schomburg Collection and is now an exhibition hall for that library.

Continue west on 135th Street

West 135th Street looking east from Seventh Avenue in 1930.

HC4 107-145 West 135th Street

(George F. Pelham, 1905-07). The change in Harlem from a community that excluded African-Americans to a community that welcomed them was expedited by the $640,000 purchase of ten tenements by St. Philip's Episcopal Church (HC10) in 1911. The buildings had previously been rented only to white tenants, but the new owner immediately sought black tenants. The households who moved into the pleasant apartments were among the first African-Americans to live in their own apartments west of Lenox Avenue. St. Philip's continued to purchase property in Harlem, becoming one of the largest land owners in the neighborhood. The church sold the 135th Street buildings in 1976. Photographer James Van Der Zee (MM3) maintained his studio in a storefronts at what is now No. 107 between 1916 and 1930.

Continue west.

HC5a YMCA, Harlem Branch

Now Jackie Robinson YMCA Youth Center, 181 West 135th Street (John F. Jackson, 1918-19) and **HC5b YMCA, Harlem Branch,** 180 West 135th Street (James C. Mackenzie, Jr., 1931-32). Like most areas of public accommodation, Ys were strictly segregated. New York's first Y for black patrons opened on West 53rd Street in 1900. Following the black migration north on Manhattan Island, a Harlem Y opened in 1919. Some African-American leaders, such as James Weldon Johnson (HC6) supported separate Ys, realizing that if there were not separate facilities for blacks and whites, there might be no Ys at all for African-Americans. In addition to the usual recreational facilities, the Harlem Y offered vocational and literacy classes, lectures, theatrical and musical performances, and community meetings and was a center of political activity. So great was the demand, that the Y soon outgrew the Italian Renaissance-inspired original building on the north side of 135th Street and a monumental new Colonial Revival structure was erected across the street. The Y was also a hotel where many migrants stayed upon their arrival in New York or where other long-time Harlemites felt at home. Among those who rented rooms here were writers Claude McKay (this was his home from 1942 to 1946), Langston Hughes (OS10), and Ralph Ellison (HH21).

Continue west.

HC6 James Weldon Johnson Apartment

187 West 135th Street (Berg & Clark, 1887). Poet, activist, and scholar James Weldon Johnson (1871-1938) lived in an apartment in this handsome

Romanesque Revival building from 1925 until his death. Johnson was born to a middle-class family in Jacksonville, Florida, but was educated in Atlanta since there were no secondary schools in Jacksonville that would accept black students. After college, he studied law, becoming the first African-American lawyer admitted to the Florida bar. Having personally seen the need for a public secondary school in Jacksonville, Johnson established one and served as the first principal. While still in Florida, Johnson wrote an opera with his brother and the poem *Lift Every Voice and Sing*, which was later set to music and became known as the Negro National Anthem.

In 1902, Johnson left Florida to study at Columbia University. While there, he wrote the campaign song, *You're All Right Teddy* for Theodore Roosevelt. This was partly responsible for his securing the post of consul to Venezuela in 1906 and Nicaragua in 1909. Returning to New York in 1914, Johnson began an association with the *New York Age*, the city's oldest black newspaper (HC13b), and with the NAACP. In 1934, Johnson became the first African-American professor at NYU. Johnson's writing about the black experience culminated with the publication of *Black Manhattan* in 1930, the first study of the history and culture of African-Americans in New York City.

Walk to the corner of West 135th Street and Adam Clayton Powell, Jr. Boulevard and look across the boulevard.

HC7   2300-2306 Adam Clayton Powell, Jr. Boulevard

Northwest corner West 135th Street (Richard Davis & Son, 1887-88). During the initial period of development in Harlem, as rowhouses were appearing on the side streets, many tenements with stores at street level were erected on the avenues. These four red brick buildings are among the most exciting surviving examples. Although apartments were not especially spacious (there were ten apartments—two per floor in each building), the facades display exuberant brickwork highlighted with ornate red terra-cotta blocks and incised stone window lintels. The buildings are crowned with spectacular iron cornices, among the best surviving in Harlem. These tenements are early works of Richard R. Davis, an architect whose practice was based in Harlem. On the side facade of No. 2300 is a carved panel announcing the Big Apple, a restaurant that occupied the space for several decades beginning in the late 1930s. The name was taken from the famous jazz expression denoting New York City.

Look diagonally across to the southwest corner.

Dancing at Small's Paradise in 1946.

HC8 Small's Paradise

2294 1/2 Adam Clayton Powell, Jr. Boulevard, southwest corner West 135th Street (H.I. Feldman, 1924-25). During the heyday of Harlem's night life, in the 1920s and 1930s, the ground floor of this commercial building housed Small's Paradise, one of the largest and most successful of Harlem's jazz clubs. When the club moved from a smaller location to this site in 1925 approximately 1500 people attended the grand opening. Small's, known as "The Hottest Spot in Harlem," was frequented by both African-American and white customers. With a band regularly led by jazz pianist Charlie Johnson, the huge crowds ate, drank, and danced to jazz well into the wee hours of the morning. In the 1960s, Small's was briefly reinvigorated under the ownership of basketball great Wilt Chamberlain who renamed the establishment "Big Wilt's Small's Paradise."

Besides Small's, this building housed many shops and offices, including those of the **Inter-State Tattler**, a popular newspaper published between about 1925 and 1932.

This paper reported on Harlem and other black communities in America, editorialized on African-American issues, described events as diverse as NAACP benefits and Harlem's famous drag balls, and published a gossip column (written in the early years of the paper by a writer known as "I. Tellonyoue"). The Greater Harlem Chamber of Commerce is discussing a restoration of this building as a center for tourism in Harlem.

Cross 135th Street and walk a short distance south.

Seventh Avenue and 135th Street in 1937. A sign in the second-story window of the building at right announces that this is the office of the "New York Amsterdam News."

HC9 *New York Amsterdam News* Office

2293 Adam Clayton Powell, Jr. Boulevard (Andrew Spence, 1885-86). Between 1916 and 1938, the *New York Amsterdam News* occupied an office on the second story of this rowhouse. James H. Anderson founded the *Amsterdam News* in 1909. Unlike the more conservative *New York Age* (HC13b), which was the city's major black newspaper in the early years of the 20th century, the *Amsterdam News* drew readers by mimicking the large headlines and tantalizing stories of the major dailies. Features often focused on African-American concerns ignored by other newspapers, including employment, civil rights, and social and political events in black neighborhoods. Although no longer housed here, the weekly *Amsterdam News* is still a major African-American journal.

Continue to the corner of West 134th Street and turn right, crossing the boulevard and walking part of the way down the next block.

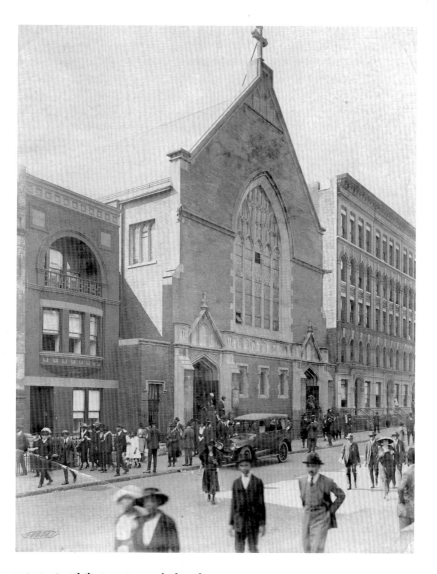

HC10 St. Philip's Episcopal Church

210-216 West 134th Street (Tandy & Foster, 1910-11).
Officially organized in 1818, St. Philip's is the oldest
African-American Episcopal congregation in New York
City. The history of the congregation echoes the devel-
opment of the city's black community. The church ini-
tially thrived under the sponsorship of liberal bishop

*St. Phillip's Episcopal
Church in the 1920s.*

John Hobart, but suffered intermittent discrimination within the Episcopal hierarchy after his death. From its original home on Centre Street, St. Philip's followed the black community north, first to Mulberry Street, then to West 25th Street, and finally to West 134th Street where property was purchased in 1909. While many Harlem landlords were unwilling to sell their property to African-Americans, they were happy to sell to the Reverend Hutchens Bishop, since they thought that this light-skinned man was white. Purchasing property in his own name and later transferring it to the church, Bishop was able to amass a considerable amount of land, including the site for a new church and a series of substantial apartment houses (HC4). The Neo-Gothic, Roman brick and terra-cotta church building was designed by two pioneering African-American architects—Vertner Tandy, the first black architect registered in New York State (HC22), and George W. Foster, Jr., one of two black architects registered in New Jersey in 1908 when that state began registration.

Return to Adam Clayton Powell, Jr. Boulevard and turn left. Walk to the corner of 135th Street and turn left.

HC11 West 135th Street and the African-American Hall of Fame

In 1995-96 the Greater Harlem Chamber of Commerce sponsored a redesign of this streetscape, including new paving and planting undertaken by the landscape architecture firm of Johansson & Walcavage. An African-American Hall of Fame has been created with plaques designed by sculptors Otto Neals and Ogundipe Fayoumi.

Continue west on 135th Street.

HC12 Florence Mills House

220 West 135th Street (G. Van Sloan, 1886-87). Florence Mills (1896-1927), who lived in this building from 1910 until her death, was probably the most famous performer of the Harlem Renaissance. Singing and dancing in musical revues, she captivated audiences in both New York and London. Mills appeared in 1923 in Noble Sissle and Eubie Blake's (HC29) *Shuffle Along*, the first Negro revue to play Broadway. Its success attracted white people to Harlem in search of the source of the

Florence Mills in "*Shuffle Along,*" 1923.

marvelous syncopated music that they had heard in the revue. During her short life as a performer, Mills had one smash hit after another. She appeared in *Plantation Revue* in New York, followed by *Dover Street to Dixie* in London. The Prince of Wales came repeatedly to see her starring in *Blackbirds of 1926*. Frail and exhausted, Mills died in New York about a month after returning from London; she was only 31 and at the height of her popularity. At her funeral, attended by 150,000 people, a plane flying low over the cemetery released a flock of blackbirds in her honor.

HC13a Frederick R. Moore House
228 West 135th Street and **HC13b New York Age Publishing Company,** 230 West 136th Street (W.P.

Anderson, 1886). Moore (1857-1943) was a civil servant who worked in the United States Department of the Treasury as an aide to seven different secretaries. He used his financial assets to help integrate Harlem as an investor in Philip Payton's Afro-American Realty Company. Moore was also involved with the National Urban League and was an owner of the *New York Age*, the major African-American newspaper in New York in the first half of the 20th century. The offices of the *Age* were located in the rowhouse next door to Moore's residence. Founded in 1887, the conservative weekly moved to Harlem in 1919 and became a powerful force in the development of Harlem as a black community, writing, in particular, for an audience of successful African-American business and professional people.

HC14 Austin Hansen Photo Studio

232 West 135th Street (W.P. Anderson, 1886). Austin Hansen (1910-1996) was a photographer whose thousands of pictures provide a record of life in Harlem from 1928 when he arrived here from the Virgin Islands until his death. After finding that a black photographer could not get a job in New York, Hansen worked at menial positions before beginning to sell photographs to the *Amsterdam News* and other African-American publications. He opened a studio in the basement of this rowhouse where he worked for 47 years. Austin Hansen, often working with his brother Aubrey, photographed black celebrities as well as average Harlem residents and recorded celebratory functions and the community's street life. His 50,000 images, now in the collection of the Schomburg Center, are an unrivaled record of 20th-century Harlem. Hansen photographs can be seen on pages 87 and 126.

Return to Adam Clayton Powell, Jr. Boulevard and turn left. Look across the boulevard to the third building north of 135th Street.

HC15 United Negro Improvement Organization (UNIA)

2305 Adam Clayton Powell, Jr. Boulevard (Andrew Spence, 1886-87). The offices of the UNIA were in this building between November, 1916 and July, 1918 and the organization's printing and publishing operations were established here in 1922. The UNIA was perhaps the most influential organization established in Harlem during the first quarter of the 20th century. Founded by Jamaican immigrant Marcus Garvey, the UNIA urged black people world wide to seize control of their destinies and improve their lives through the control of their own businesses. Garvey also preached a Pan-African philosophy that had as its central premise the return of black people to Africa. He was able to sell stock to finance the Black Star Shipping Line, on which he hoped to transport people back to the African continent. Although Garvey was deported from the United States in 1927 following a conviction for mail fraud, his views of racial solidarity and economic strength had a tremendous impact on black people throughout the nation.

Also in this building was **Bessie Delany's Dental Office.** Dr. Bessie Delany, who, along with her sister Sadie are the subject of the best-selling memoir *Having Our Say*, joined her brother in practice here in 1925.

HC16 New York Urban League Manhattan Branch

Walk to West 136th Street and turn left.

202-206 West 136th Street (Frederick G. Butcher, 1889-90). The National Urban League was founded in 1911 to focus on several issues beyond the direct purview of the NAACP. Employment equity, health, and social conditions in American cities were to be the concerns on which the Urban League would commit its energies. William Bulkley, the first vice-chairman of the Urban League summarized its goals in a 1909 speech: "We do not ask for charity, all we ask is opportunity. We do not beg for alms; we beg for a chance." The need for this biracial organization became increasingly apparent as poor, rural, African-Americans from the South moved to New York and other northern cities. In 1917, these three rowhouses became the League's Manhattan branch office. Other social-service organizations also occupied space in the buildings, including the Harlem Tuberculosis and Health Committee and the North Harlem Center of the Henry Street Settlement's Visiting Nurses Service.

Continue to the middle of the block so that you will have a good overview of the rowhouses.

The New York Urban League's offices in c.1940.

HC17a 202-266 West 136th Street

(Frederick G. Butcher, 1889-90) and **HC17b 203-267 West 136th Street** (Thomas C. Van Brunt, 1891-95). In the late 1880s and early 1890s speculative developers in Harlem frequently purchased entire blockfronts and erected long unified rows; there were 33 individual houses in each of these rows. The more interesting of the two is that to the north. Architect/builder Thomas C. Van Brunt purchased the property in 1891 and planned a series of relatively narrow dwellings (16 or 17 feet wide) for people of moderate means who would provide small down payments. Although Van Brunt clearly designed this row as a single unified blockfront, he created a dynamic streetscape by employing a variety of materials in different colors and textures (unfortunately, many of the houses have been painted); several types of sandstone and different types of brick were used. He also provided varied roof profiles (false mansards and pyramidal towers), different cornice designs, and a rich vocabulary of ornamental details. Note, for example, the carved pediments at the entrances to Nos. 245 and 247; the stylized Byzantine foliate carving at Nos. 225 and 227; and the naturalistic leaves at Nos. 229-235. Many houses in the Van Brunt row retain stained-glass windows, but the most interesting stained glass can be seen on the Butcher row. In the transoms of Nos. 234-240 and the large arched window of No. 220 are vibrantly-colored panels of Belcher Mosaic Glass, a type of stained glass composed of small triangular tesserae highlighted by rounded "jewels." This type of glass is discussed in more detail on the Hamilton Heights Tour (HH28).

Sadly, the house on this block with the greatest cul-

Four of the Van Brunt houses on the north side of West 136th Street, 1892.

tural significance has been demolished. This was No. 267, a rooming house run by Iolanthe Sydney, which has been called "the headquarters of the Harlem Renaissance's vanguard wing." Sydney provided free rooms to indigent artists including painters Aaron Douglas and Bruce Nugent and writers Wallace Thurman, Langston Hughes (OS10), and Zora Neale Hurston. Hurston dubbed the dwelling "Niggerati Manor." Many of the residents, including Thurman and Nugent, were gay and Nugent painted a series of homoerotic murals on the walls.

Two houses on this block are of special historical interest:

Brotherhood of Sleeping Car Porters Headquarters (BSCP) 239 West 136th Street. For a few years, beginning in 1929, this building housed the headquarters of the first African-American labor union in America, A. Philip Randolph's Brotherhood of Sleeping Car Porters. The BSCP was a significant force for black unity, equal employment opportunity, and wage equity. With most unions excluding African-Americans, the BSCP, whose membership was made up of thousands of railroad service workers, gave the black worker an active voice in the political arena and nurtured political activism. The late 1920s and early 1930s was a difficult period for the BSCP as it struggled with the Pullman Company for official recognition (only granted in 1937). Several years after moving onto 136th Street, funds were so depleted that Randolph and his organization were evicted and all of their records thrown onto the street. Through his union activities, A. Philip Randolph became a leader in the fight of civil rights. He was instrumental in forcing Franklin D. Roosevelt to desegregate defense industries and in persuading Harry Truman to desegregate the military.

White Rose Mission 262 West 136th Street. From about 1918 until 1967 this was the home of the White Rose Mission one of the most important social service providers in the black community. When unsuspecting young women sought to leave the south during the early years of the 20th century, they were often lured north with promises of jobs by unscrupulous employment agents. After signing contracts, the women were at the mercy of these men who had paid for their transportation. Victoria Earle Matthews (1861-1907) sought to protect and educate these young women as they made they way to a new life. Matthews was born a slave in Georgia. Although she received little formal schooling, she loved to read and taught herself to write. Her essays and articles were published in some of the major newspapers and magazines of the period. Matthews's greatest passion was for public service within the black community of New York. This zeal led her to found the White Rose Mission, providing a "Christian, non-sectarian Home for Colored Girls and Women, where they may be trained in the principles of practical self-help and right living."

Return to the corner of West 136th Street and Adam Clayton Powell, Jr. Boulevard.

HC18 Ferdinand Q. Morton Apartment

201 West 136th Street (aka 2320 Adam Clayton Powell, Jr. Boulevard), northwest corner West 136th Street (Neville & Bagge, 1897-98). During the 1920s, one apartment in this building was the home of Ferdinand Q. Morton, a leading political figure in Harlem. Morton was one of the first black New Yorkers appointed to a major city agency, becoming a Civil Service Commissioner in 1922. He was given this position by Democrat Charles F. Murphy, a Tammany Hall politician. Morton wielded a small amount of power in the Tammany machine, mostly through his relationship with Murphy and was able to secure city positions for a few other African-Americans.

HC19 203-231 and 202-252 West 137th Street

(John Hauser, 1897-1903). John Hauser was a prolific designer of speculative rowhouses who moved his office from Yorkville to Harlem in 1900. The 41 houses Hauser designed on this street (15 on the north side and 26 on the south) were built in seven separate units over the course of six years. They create what may be the city's most dramatic "stoopscape." Every single high stoop with stone side walls is extant! Most are anchored by stone newel posts crowned with carved caps. The regularity of the rowhouses designed by Hauser reflect the

Turn left on Adam Clayton Powell, Jr. Boulevard and walk to the corner of West 137th Street. Turn left and walk part of the way down the block.

taste, at the turn-of-the-century, for carefully balanced Renaissance-inspired compositions. The stone carvings, probably created by anonymous Italian immigrants, are exceptionally fine, especially at the base of the rounded oriels projecting from most facades.

In 1916, St. James Presbyterian Church (HH6) purchased No. 206 and for many years it was home to the church's rectors, including the **Reverend Dr. William Lloyd Imes** who, during the 1920s and 1930s, was a distinguished community activist, particularly concerned about employment issues in the African-American community. He was a union advocate and was active in the fight against job discrimination. Adam Clayton Powell, Jr. described Imes as "a great man, with the mind of a scholar, the soul of a saint, the heart of a brother, the tongue of a prophet, and the hand of a militant." For many years, two of the dwellings on the north side housed self-help and social organizations established by immigrants from the West Indies — No. 207 was home to the Montserrat Society and No. 211 has housed the Nassau Bahamas Association. Note the beautifully-carved modern doors with African themes at No. 213.

Return to Adam Clayton Powell, Jr. Boulevard and turn left; look across the street.

HC20 Renaissance Theater and Renaissance Ballroom and Casino

2341-2359 Adam Clayton Powell, Jr. Boulevard between West 137th and West 138th streets (Harry Creighton Ingalls, Theater: 1920-21; Ballroom/casino: 1922-23). The Renaissance was one of the major venues for exciting night life in Harlem from the 1920s through the 1950s and it is one of the few major Harlem Renaissance-era night spots still standing. Established by realtor William Roche, an immigrant from Montserrat, the "Renny" offered dancing, cabaret acts, and jazz, hosting many of the finest bands of the 1920s, 1930s, and 1940s, including those of Vernon Andrade, Fletcher Henderson (HC22), Chick Webb, Edgar Hayes, and Al Sears.

The Renaissance Casino was famous as the home of the Harlem Renaissance basketball team, affectionately known as the "Rens" or "Rennies." In 1922, Bob Dou-

Fashionably dressed Harlem residents strolling by the Renaissance Ballroom on Seventh Avenue. The poster seeking the reelection of Mayor James J. Walker dates this view to 1929.

glas, a migrant from St. Kitts, asked Roche to sponsor a basketball team that would play at the Casino, offering to name the team after the establishment. On November 30, 1923, the Rens, the first professional team of black basketball players, debuted. The team played on the dance floor of the Casino's ballroom with portable baskets. The Rens racked up a phenomenal record; when it disbanded in the 1940s it had won 2,588 games and lost only 592. The two-building Renaissance complex is faced with multi-colored brick, highlighted with decorative terra cotta and especially unusual tile trim. The Abyssinian Development Corporation is planning a rehabilitation of the building.

The Harlem Rennies in the 1920s with inset of founder Bob Douglas.

Walk to the middle of the block.

United Colored Democracy's office in 1938.

Continue north to West 139th Street. As you walk, notice the rear alley running through the block between West 138th and 139th streets. Turn left on West 139th Street and walk part of the way down the block to get the general feel of this extraordinary architectural ensemble.

HC21 United Colored Democracy Headquarters (UCD)

2352 Adam Clayton Powell, Jr. Boulevard (James Brown Lord, 1891-93). Beginning in about 1925, this former single-family rowhouse contained the headquarters of United Colored Democracy, the segregated section of the Democratic Party in New York, organized in 1898 at a time when the Democrats excluded black people from regular membership. The founder, W.I.R. Richardson, an immigrant from the island of St. Kitts, was interested in making party politics more responsive to the black community. While most African-Americans who voted during the early 20th century turned to the Republicans, the party of Lincoln, many West Indian immigrants were willing to try the Democratic Party with its lure of patronage jobs. Ferdinand Q. Morton (HC18) became the leader of UCD in 1915.

King Model Houses (Striver's Row): Part I (HC22-23)

The 146 rowhouses and three apartment buildings of the King Model Houses constitute two of the most spectacular streetscapes in New York City. The successful building contractor David H. King, Jr. purchased property on West 138th and 139th streets in 1890 from the Equitable Life Assurance Society. King planned a residential project that would appeal to people of moderate means, arguing that "the homes of New Yorkers [should] be sunny, tasteful, convenient, and commodious even if their occupants are not millionaires." He erected houses with fine exterior materials and carefully planned interior layouts complete with elegant woodwork, modern plumbing, and other conveniences. King was able to acquire products of high quality at reasonable prices because he purchased all items in bulk.

The creation of a unified ensemble was important to King, but he sought to avoid the monotony of less sophisticated rowhouse designs. To create variety, he commissioned rows from three of New York's most tal-

Drawing of the rear alley of the King Model Houses, 1892. The fountain was never constructed.

73

206-208 West 139th Street, part of Bruce Price's King Model Houses row in c. 1940.

ented architects. Although each row consists of between 25 and 35 houses, ranging in width from 17' to 23', they are anything but boring. The 775 foot long block-fronts are interrupted by cross streets that break the rows into smaller units. In addition, subtle variations in the massing, notably projecting central and end pavilions, augment the lively designs. The cross streets, with their handsome iron gates, lead to rear alleys that are among the most significant aspects of the project. Unlike Washington and Philadelphia, New York was not planned with alleys for service deliveries and the collection of garbage. Thus, streets are often dirty and clogged with delivery vehicles. Addressing this problem, King replaced the private rear yards common on New York rowhouses with service alleys.

Although King was able to create a superb residential neighborhood, the project was not a financial success;

only nine houses sold. Perhaps potential buyers were unimpressed by the novel alleys, preferring, instead, the private rear yards provided by other local developers. In 1895, a national economic depression resulted in King ceding the remaining houses to the mortgagee, Equitable Life. Equitable rented the dwellings, selling 31 in 1905, but holding the remainder until 1919-20 when they were sold to black buyers. The changing character of the community residing at the King Model Houses is discussed on West 138th Street (HC29).

Stanford White's King Model Houses row in the 1920s.

HC22a 202-252 West 139th Street
(Bruce Price and Clarence S. Luce, 1891-93) and
HC22b 203-269 West 139th Street (McKim, Mead & White; Stanford White, partner in charge, 1891-93). The houses on the south side of the street are traditional New York rowhouses with high stoops and parlor-floor entrances. They are early examples of Colonial Revival

design and are a reflection of a new interest among architects in the nation's Colonial heritage. Although the yellow brick houses with white terra-cotta trim are quite narrow (most are only 17' wide), the high paired stoops create the illusion of wider buildings. Note the handsome iron railings and the solid, triple-paneled oak doors that remain unaltered at eight entrances.

The 32 rowhouses designed by Stanford White on the north side of the street form the most sophisticated blockfront of the King Model Houses. The Italian Renaissance-inspired buildings are faced with rusticated sandstone and rose-colored iron spot bricks bound by pink mortar and trimmed with terra cotta. Unlike the traditional high stoop houses designed by Price, White chose the innovative American basement plan, with the entry at street level. This is a remarkably early use of this plan and an indication of the declining popularity of the stoop among sophisticated architects. The symmetrical row pivots on the central house at No. 233 with its entrance recessed within an arcaded loggia.

In the 1920s and 1930s, several of the houses on this block were owned or rented to prominent African-American professionals or successful entertainment and sports figures. Note, in particular the following homes:

Vertner Tandy House, 221 West 139th Street. Vertner Tandy (1885-1949), who lived here from 1919 until his death, was the first African-American architect licensed in New York State. He studied at the Tuskegee Institute and graduated from the Cornell University School of Architecture in 1908. Among Tandy's best works are St. Philip's Episcopal Church (HC10) and the Villa Lewaro in Irvington, the home of hair-products magnate, Madame C.J. Walker, the first black woman millionaire in America.

W.C. Handy House, 232 West 139th Street. After getting his start as a coronet player with traveling minstrel shows, W.C. Handy (1873-1958) became a collector and compiler of the African-American folk music tradition. Often called "the father of the blues," Handy traveled throughout the South, translating the oral traditions of blues and spirituals into musical notation. Without his dedication to this tradition, much of this music might have been lost. Handy was also a composer of spirituals and hymns, as well as such popular tunes as *The Old Miss Rag* (1916) and *The Atlanta Blues* (1923). Handy owned this house from 1919 until 1922.

Fletcher Henderson House, 228 West 139th Street. When Fletcher Henderson (1897-1952) arrived in New York City in 1920 it was to pursue his education as a scientist. However, with years of classical piano study, Henderson landed jobs in the music business, first with the Pace-Handy Company (founded by Harry Pace and W.C. Handy in 1918) and later with Black Swan Records (HC29). As an orchestra leader and jazz pianist, Henderson and his musicians perfected an exciting style of jazz that was more rhythmic than earlier jazz. His orchestra (see photo, p.24) included such famous musicians as Don Redman and Louis Armstrong. After purchasing this house in 1924, Henderson was able to walk to his gigs at Harlem's best jazz clubs.

Harry Wills House, 245 West 139th Street. Harry Wills (1892-1958) was a top contender to the heavyweight boxing title during the first quarter of the 20th century, but, due to racism in the boxing world was never able to actually fight for the honor. From 1908 to 1915, the heavyweight title was held by African-American boxer Jack Johnson. Johnson was hated by most white boxing fans and each of his challengers was considered a "great white hope." Johnson finally lost a match to Jess Willard in a 1915 fight in Cuba. Neither Willard nor Jack Dempsey, his successor as heavyweight champion, would fight a black man since fight promoters were not anxious to permit another black fighter to earn the title. Indeed, Dempsey paid Wills a forfeit of $50,000 rather than fight him for the title. Wills owned this house between 1922 and 1930. In 1925, he lived here with his wife and a maid; at the time, it was one of the few single-family residences on the block. After retiring from box-

Harry Wills in training, 1927.

Walk to the corner of Frederick Douglass Boulevard.

Cross Frederick Douglass Boulevard and continue walking west. Note the vista towards Shepard Hall at City College (HH9).

ing, Wills invested in real estate, managing several Harlem apartment buildings.

HC23 King Model Houses Apartments

267 West 139th Street (McKim, Mead & White, 1891-93) and 272 West 139th Street (Bruce Price and Clarence S. Luce, 1891-93). On the corners of Eighth Avenue, immediately adjacent to the noisy and dirty elevated rail line, King built four-story apartment buildings, each originally with six units. The designs of these buildings complement those of the adjoining rowhouses.

HC24 305-321 West 139th Street

(Arthur F. DeSaldern, 1896-97). The short blocks between Frederick Douglass Boulevard and Edgecombe Avenue form an enclave that was developed in the late 1880s and 1890s with relatively modest rowhouses of great charm. The designers of most of these houses were obscure architects with small practices. Nonetheless, they often created work of great interest. DeSaldern's row of ten simple Neo-Renaissance houses illustrates the growing popularity of white limestone from Indiana as a building material during the 1890s.

HC25 Lenox Presbyterian Church

Now Grace Congregational Church, 310 West 139th Street (Joseph Ireland, 1892-93). The growth of the Lenox Presbyterian Church reflects the rapid development of this section of Harlem. A Presbyterian Sunday School was opened on Eighth Avenue and 137th Street in 1890 and it grew so fast that a church congregation was organized and this small Romanesque Revival chapel erected. By 1905, the congregation had outgrown the building and moved to a larger church on St. Nicholas Avenue and West 141st Street (HH6). The 139th Street building was sold to a Swedish church which remained here until 1923. In that year, it became home to its present occupant, a Congregational church with a black membership. Although a simple inexpensive structure, the brick on the facade is employed with great subtlety; note how bricks are laid on end to create arches and how

the brick at the windows and along the gable projects
slightly.

HC26 St. Mark's Methodist Church

Edgecombe Avenue, southwest corner West 138th Street
(Sibley & Fetherston, 1921-26). St. Mark's has long been
one of the most prominent African-American churches
in New York City. At the turn-of-the-century, St. Mark's
was located on West 53rd Street, but opened a storefront mission, the Salem Church, to minister to what was
then a small black community in Harlem. Following a
1900 riot in the Tenderloin in which African-Americans
were randomly beaten by police and marauding gangs,
St. Mark's minister Reverend Dr. W.H. Brooks became an
outspoken community leader. He later became a founder
of the NAACP and the National Urban League. When St.
Mark's moved to Harlem, this magnificent Neo-Gothic
style church complex was constructed to house the congregation.

HC27a 309-325 West 138th Street

(Edwin R. Will, 1889-90) and **HC27b 304-318 West
138th Street** (J. Averit Webster, 1896). Like Arthur
DeSaldern (HC24), Edwin Will and J. Averit Webster are
representative of the hundreds of architects who maintained small-scale practices in New York City in the late
19th century. A comparison between these two rows
illustrates the change in architectural taste between the
late 1880s when Will designed the Queen Anne row on
the north side of the street and the mid 1890s when
Webster designed the Neo-Renaissance row to the south.
Will's row has the quirky exuberance popular during the
1880s. The oriels, decorative terra-cotta panels, and massive L-shaped stone stoops create lively facades, while the
gables, gablettes, and corner tower offer a dynamic silhouette. Webster's work is far more subdued, reflecting
a new interest in the regularity and balance of Renaissance design. Instead of the dark red brick and stone used
by Will, Webster chose lighter-hued materials—a yellow
iron-spot brick and white limestone. Ornament is
derived from Renaissance precedents, notably the deep

Continue walking
west. Note the
rowhouses at Nos.
314-322
designed by John
Hauser in 1904
that closely resem-
ble those seen on
West 137th Street
(HC19). Turn left
on Edgecombe
Avenue and walk
to 138th Street.

Turn left onto West
138th Street.

Continue east to Frederick Douglass Boulevard. Note the St. Charles Condominiums (The Stephen B. Jacobs Group,1993-95), an affordable infill housing project that successfully maintains the scale of the earlier rowhouses. Cross the street and continue east on 138th Street.

cornices and the tripartite Palladian window arrangements on the third story with their urns, vines, and shells.

HC28 252 West 138th Street

Later Coachmen's Union League Society of New York City/Now Victory Tabernacle Seventh-Day Christian Church, (Jardine, Kent & Jardine, 1895-96). This joyous little building never fails to surprise, although just why the architects designed a limestone and marble structure that resembles a palace on a canal in Venice remains a mystery. Initially planned for offices, the building was sold in 1923 to the Coachmen's Union League Society, which was, apparently, a social and self-help organization for coachmen and chauffeurs. They lost the building in a foreclosure action in 1928. The Victory Tabernacle has occupied the building since 1942.

The members of the Coachmen's Union League Society pose for a picture in 1924. Photo by James Van Der Zee.

The interior of one of James Brown Lord's units at the King Model Houses, 1892

King Model Houses (Striver's Row) Part II (HC29a & HC29b)

HC29a 202-250 West 138th Street

(James Brown Lord, 1891-93) and **HC29b 203-271 West 138th Street** (Bruce Price and Clarence S. Luce, 1891-93). This is the second street developed by David King as part of his model housing project. The red brick houses with brownstone trim on the south side are the widest in the King complex; all are over 20' wide. Of the three facade designs built by King, this is the most conservative, displaying the dark-hued materials and L-shaped stoops popular in the 1880s. Note the entrances to the side alleys with signs that announce that these are private roads and entreat entrants to walk their horses.

Who Lived in the King Model Houses?

Since King had been able to sell only a few of the houses before foreclosure, the Equitable Life Assurance Company rented the dwellings. The 1900 census records that the residents were just the type of white middle-class business and professional people that King had sought as purchasers. Most households had between five and ten residents, including one or two servants. A typical example is No. 238 which, in 1900 was rented by William Silverman, a 56-year-old German-Jewish immigrant who manufactured suspenders in a factory on West 14th

Street. He lived here with his wife (a native New York), their three children, his mother-in-law, a Swedish cook, and an Irish chambermaid.

By 1915, a number of the houses had two families. While many residents were born in the United States, there were also many immigrants — from Russia, Poland, Germany, Ireland, and England. There were also several homes occupied by people from Colombia who had moved to New York as a result of increasing business connections resulting from the construction of the Panama Canal. This development was striking enough to prompt the *New York Times* to print an article entitled "Latin-Americans in Harlem Block" in 1913.

The *African-American* Presence and the Evolution of Striver's Row

Despite the fact that the first tenements in Harlem rented to black households were located near the King Model Houses, Equitable Life would not rent to African-Americans. As the white population on surrounding blocks declined, Equitable divested itself of Harlem properties and in 1919-20, as the leases of the white renters expired, the houses were sold to individual black owners, most of whom were already Harlem residents. Some of the houses were sold to successful African-American professionals, including doctors and dentists, and others became home to prominent entertainment and sports figures. These, however, were the exception. Most of the new owners were working people, striving to survive in a discriminatory society. By the 1930s, the King Houses had been dubbed "Striver's Row," a reference to the efforts of residents to attain a middle-class lifestyle.

With their sale to African-Americans, most of the rowhouses were converted into rooming houses. While three to five lodgers was typical on these blocks, in 1925, No. 247 housed Anna Hames and her daughter, plus 15 lodgers! Evidence of the potential problems created by lodgers is found in the rules of the Kings Court Association, a home-owners group established in the 1920s. The rules entreated owners to hang uniform "room-for-rent" signs and warned lodgers against leaning out of windows or undressing without pulling down their shades. "Remember," stated the rules, "'Eternal Vigilance' is the price; the 'Block Beautiful' is your reward." Most of the new residents, both owners and boarders, were American-born, but there were also many immigrants from the West Indies. The new residents held jobs reflecting the severely limited professional opportunities open to black people in the North. Most of the men were service employees, including many red caps, Pullman porters, and other railroad workers, as well as hotel bellmen, barbers, waiters, and elevator operators, while women were often sales ladies, launderers, dressmakers, or domestic servants. Among Anna Hames' lodgers were four waiters, a Pullman porter, a bellman, a chauffeur, two messengers, and a clerk. Six of the lodgers were from the Caribbean (Jamaica, Grenada, British Guiana, and Puerto Rico).

As you walk down the street, note the following houses of historic interest:

Black Swan Record Company, 257 West 138th Street. Harry Pace, who lived here between 1919 and 1925, founded the Black Swan Record Company in 1921, opening offices in his basement. Pace saw a need for a company that would record the voices and instrumental arrangements of African-American musicians at a time when few recording studios made records of black performers. Black Swan proved that there was a market for these artists. For several years, Black Swan issued about twelve records a month by such performers as Fletcher Henderson (HC22), Ethel Waters, The Harmony Five, and Florence Cole Talbert. Ironically, the success of Black Swan led to its demise since mainstream companies began regularly recording black performers.

Black Swan's label for Down Home Blues *as recorded by Ethel Waters and the Jazz Masters.*

James Dickson Carr House, 238 West 138th Street. James Dickson Carr (1868-1920) was the first black graduate of Rutgers and then continued his studies at the Columbia University School of Law. He was involved with the early development of the United Colored

Democracy (HC21) and was one of the first African-Americans to receive a non-menial government job, working as an assistant district attorney from 1897-1900 and in the corporation council's office from 1904-1920.

Noble Sissle (left) and Eubie Blake in 1927.

Eubie Blake House, 236 West 138th Street. The pianist and songwriter Eubie Blake (1883-1983) lived in this house between 1921 and 1945. Blake and his partner Noble Sissle were the team responsible for some of the most popular songs and musicals of the 1920s and 1930s. Sissle and Blake began their careers in vaudeville as the "Dixie Duo." In 1921 they composed their first musical, *Shuffle Along*. Starring Florence Mills (HC12), the show opened on Broadway to rave reviews establishing the rage for black-themed musicals. Among the great songs for which Blake wrote the music are *I'm Just Wild About Harry, You Were Meant For Me*, and *Memories of You*.

Will Marion Cook House, 221 West 138th Street. Will Marion Cook (1869-1944), one of America's greatest conductors and composers, lived here from 1918 until his death. Cook studied at Oberlin Preparatory School Conservatory in Ohio, with Josef Joachim in Berlin, and with Antonin Dvořák, during the Czech composer's residence in New York. Dvořák's understanding of American music, evident, for example, in his *New World*

Symphony, was influenced by Cook. Cook's first orchestra, the New York Syncopated Orchestra, toured the country in 1910. He later became an arranger for the Clef Club Orchestra led by James Reese Europe. Among Cook's most famous compositions are *Swing Along* and *Rain Song*. Cook was a mentor and teacher for many of the Harlem Renaissance musicians and was considered one of the "dads" of jazz.

Dr. Louis T. Wright House, 218 West 138th Street. In 1920, this became the home of Dr. Louis T. Wright (1891-1952), a pioneering black surgeon. A graduate of Harvard Medical School (he was fourth in his class), Wright fought prejudice throughout his career. With the assistance of Civil Service Commissioner Ferdinand Q. Morton (HC18), Wright and a small number of other physicians were admitted to practice at Harlem Hospital; Wright later became the hospital's administrator. As a researcher, Wright proved that the Schick test for diphtheria was equally valuable to people with dark and light skin, despite allegations that African-Americans could not benefit from it because of their skin color. He was also the first African-American physician to have his work published in a major mainstream medical text. In addition to his medical career, Wright was active in the broader Civil Rights Movement, serving as chairman of the board of the NAACP for twenty years.

Alpha Phi Alpha Fraternity, 203 West 138th Street. For several years in the 1920s, this was the fraternity house of the Eta Chapter of Alpha Phi Alpha, the oldest African-American fraternity in the country. The fraternity was founded at Cornell in 1905, with the New York chapter organized in 1909. Among the founders of the fraternity was Vertner Tandy (HC22) who also designed the fraternity's pin. College fraternities served several important functions for young African-American men, providing a forum for leadership training when other avenues were closed to them and a refuge from the barrage of prejudice, racial epithets, and demeaning textbooks that many experienced.

Walk to the corner and cross Adam Clayton Powell, Jr. Boulevard; continue east on West 138th Street, taking a close look at the Renaissance Casino (HC20) as you walk past.

The *Alpha Phi Alpha* basketball team poses on the stoop of 203 West 138th Street in 1926. Photo by James Van Der Zee.

HC30 Abyssinian Baptist Church

136-142 West 138th Street (Charles W. Bolton & Son, 1922-23). Abyssinian Baptist Church, named for the ancient land of Ethiopia, was founded in 1808 on Worth Street in Manhattan. One of New York's oldest African-American congregations, its history has reflected the growth and residential patterns of the black community expanding from a tiny wooden building in Lower Manhattan to an imposing Neo-Gothic structure in Harlem. In 1908, the dynamic preacher Adam Clayton Powell, Sr. (HH25) became minister and he began preaching sermons urging his flock to move to Harlem. Powell became well known for a "social gospel" that combined concern for the spirit with social activism. Powell retired in 1938 and his successor to the pulpit was his son, Adam Clayton Powell, Jr. who, in 1944, became

The interior of the Abyssinian Baptist Church with a full congregation. Photo by Austin Hansen.

Harlem's first black congressman.

The present church was constructed during the tenure of Adam Clayton Powell, Sr. Unlike St. Philip's (HC10) and Mother A.M.E. Zion (HC32) which commissioned designs from black architects, Abyssinian Baptist was designed by a firm of white architects from Philadelphia that specialized in Protestant church design.

HC31 Alberta Hunter Apartment

133 West 138th Street. The great blues singer Alberta Hunter (1895-1984; see photo p.88) lived in this building in 1931-32. It was one of several Harlem apartments that she occupied for brief periods. Hunter enjoyed a long and successful career writing songs, performing in clubs with such musicians as Fletcher Henderson and Louis Armstrong, and appearing on television. Hunter began her career in Chicago about 1914, but quickly moved to the blues and jazz clubs of Harlem. Her 1922 composition *Downhearted Blues* became a hit when recorded by Bessie Smith the following year. Hunter entertained troops during World War II and the Korean War and continued to record and entertain in clubs until her death.

HC32 Mother A.M.E. Zion Church

140-148 West 137th Street (George W. Foster, Jr.,

Returning to Adam Clayton Powell, Jr. Boulevard and turn left. Walk to 137th Street and turn left.

Portrait of Alberta Hunter. Photo by James C. Campbell.

To return to the Schomburg Center or the corner of Lenox Avenue and West 135th Street, go back to Adam Clayton Powell, Jr. Boulevard, turn left and walk two blocks to West 135th Street. Turn left and walk to the next corner.

1923-25). Mother A.M.E. Zion, a congregation famous for its long history of activism, was founded in 1796 by some of the most prominent African-American families in the city. During the years of slavery in the United States, many African-American churches in the A.M.E. Zion (African Methodist Episcopal Zion) conference, including Mother Zion, participated in the clandestine Underground Railroad by sheltering runaway slaves. Such churches earned the name "freedom churches." In the early 20th century, Mother Zion followed the movement of African-American resettlement to Harlem. Architect George W. Foster, Jr., one of the first black architects to be registered in the United States, designed the Neo-Gothic church. Throughout the twentieth century, Mother Zion's congregation has continued to practice a liberation theology, providing for the sick and needy, participating in civil rights protests, and urging members to be politically active.

Hamilton Heights/ Sugar Hill Tour

Introduction

Located approximately nine miles north of the Battery, the heights overlooking Central Harlem became a popular venue for country homes erected by wealthy New Yorkers in the 18th and early 19th centuries. This walk encompasses two early 19th-century estates—Alexander Hamilton's "Grange" generally the area south of West 145th Street, and Samuel Bradhurst's "Pinehurst" to the north. Each estate centered on an elegant Federal style house. By the mid 19th century, the area was attracting charitable and educational institutions—a large property south of 136th Street became the Convent of the Sacred Heart (the derivation of Convent Avenue's name); in 1897 City College acquired land immediately to the north. After the Civil War, land speculation increased in northern Manhattan and this area, variously referred to at the time as St. Nicholas Heights, Hamilton Heights, and Convent Hill, became increasingly desirable for residence.

The opening of the elevated railroad on Eighth Avenue in 1879, with stations at 135th and 145th streets, created opportunities for development on both the Grange and Pinehurst estates. Some properties near the edge of the cliff were sold in the 1880s for the construction of suburban villas, but most of the land awaited the arrival of speculative rowhouse builders. William H. De Forest and his son William H. De Forest, Jr. were responsible for much of the development south of 145th Street. William De Forest purchased the Grange property in several transactions in the 1870s and early 1880s. He gave the Grange mansion to St. Luke's Church and had it moved, in order to save it from demolition as he developed the property. The De Forests laid out streets and planned a development restricted to single-family homes that, according to an 1886 article in the *Real Estate Record*

Nineteenth-century photograph of Pinehurst, the Bradhurst family's mansion.

and *Builders Guide*, "will certainly have a strong distinctive character of its own, though bearing more resemblance to the suburbs of London than to anything in the vicinity of New York."

Residential improvements on the Bradhurst property occurred somewhat later than those on the Grange. Henry M. Bradhurst began selling the family's land in the 1870s, but the depressed real estate market during much of that decade meant that most lots did not leave Bradhurst ownership until the 1880s. Major rowhouse development began in the following decade. By the early 20th century, most rowhouse construction had ended in the tour area, but apartment houses appeared on vacant parcels or replaced suburban villas.

Early residents of the new rowhouses tended to be middle-class professional people and their families. Owners were white, mostly native-born Protestants (accounting for the fine Protestant churches on the tour), but there were also a smaller number of immigrant owners, mostly from Germany, Italy, and Ireland. It was not until the late 1920s and 1930s, as the expanding black population increased pressure on Harlem's housing

Sketch of 452-466
West 144th Street
(HH15a), 1890.

stock, that prosperous black households moved to the
Heights. The area soon became known as "Sugar Hill."

"Sugar Hill" refers to a place where those with
"sugar" (that is, money) settled. Many of the African-
Americans who moved here were not seeking refuge
from crowded tenements in the Tenderloin or Central
Harlem or from deplorable conditions in the South.
Instead, they were artists, writers, and musicians, government workers, and professionals who had been able,
despite the prejudice within American society, to secure
incomes that placed them within the middle class. Some
of the residents were inter-racial couples who found that
a black neighborhood was the only place in which they
could feel comfortable and would be accepted. Some
middle-class blacks purchased the neighborhood's fine
rowhouses, while others rented apartments. The most
prestigious addresses were 409 and 555 Edgecombe
Avenue (HH31 and JT11), twelve-story apartment
houses with breathtaking views. Of course, not everyone
found Sugar Hill an ideal place to live. Claude McKay
noted in 1940 that "Sugar Hill has the reputation of
being the romping ground of the fashionable set. The
houses on the hill are more modern, but rents are exor-
bitant.... Sugar Hill is vinegar sour to many of its residents pinching themselves to meet the high rent." Still,
its fine rowhouses and apartments, famous residents, and
scenic location made it a desirable place for affluent
African-Americans to live.

As you will see, the Hamilton Heights/Sugar Hill area
is still a beautiful place to live. The early portion of this
walk wends its way in and out of the Hamilton Heights
Historic District, designated by the New York City Landmarks Preservation Commission in 1974. There are also
several individual landmarks discussed on the tour.
Ongoing efforts to expand historic district designations
have yet to bear fruit.

Original design of St.
Luke's Episcopal
Church (HH1) with
planned tower, 1891.

Tour

Begin: Southwest corner of Convent Avenue and West 141st Street

HH1   St. Luke's Episcopal Church

285 Convent Avenue, northeast corner West 141st Street (R.H. Robertson, 1891-92). The austere St. Luke's, with its two shades of rough-textured stone and its bold round arches, is one New York City's finest essays in the Romanesque Revival style. The congregation's roots extend to the organization of a small parish in Greenwich Village in 1820 and the construction of what is now St. Luke's-in-the-Fields on Hudson Street. By the early 1890s much of the congregation had moved uptown and the parish followed. Built on a steeply sloping site, Robertson's church is composed of a series of clearly articulated masses—tall nave, side aisles, transepts, porch, chimney, apse, etc. The church was never completed—a tall tower is missing and close examination will reveal that the column capitals on the porch were never carved.

Cross West 141st Street and walk north to the middle of the block.

HH2   280-298 Convent Avenue

(Henri Fouchaux, 1899-1902). The entire blockfront across from St. Luke's is lined with a dynamic row of Beaux-Arts rowhouses faced in limestone. The sculptural quality of Beaux-Arts design (named for the Ecole des Beaux-Arts, the great Parisian architecture school) is apparent in the carving on these buildings, especially in the use of cartouches. Cartouches are the shield-like forms evident, in particular, on the second-story of Nos. 284 and 294, that are a key ornamental feature on most Beaux-Arts buildings. Note the high stone stoops. These houses are late examples of the use of the stoop, an entrance feature that typifies 19th-century New York rowhouses, but which was losing popularity in the 1890s as will be seen around the corner (HH4).

HH3   The Grange

Now Hamilton Grange National Monument, 287 Convent Avenue (John McComb, Jr., 1801-02). In 1798, Alexander Hamilton conceived of a "sweet project," buying land in northern Manhattan and building a home

Hamilton Grange on its original site with grove of thirteen gum trees at right.

for his family. The result was the Grange, named for his ancestral manor in Scotland. The simple yet elegant Federal style house was originally surrounded by extensive gardens, including a famous grove of 13 gum trees, representing the original colonies, a gift from George Washington (these survived until 1912 when they were cut down for development). Hamilton was killed in a duel with Aaron Burr only two years after completing the house. In 1889, as rowhouse development was beginning to transform the former Hamilton estate, developer William De Forest donated the Grange to St. Luke's Church. The house was moved from Convent Avenue and 143rd Street, realigned with a side elevation facing the street, and shorn of its original porch. Services were held in the house while the new church was under construction. It served as a rectory until 1924 when it was sold to the American Scenic and Historic Preservation Society, one of the first organizations in the nation involved with architectural preservation; the property was taken over by the National Park Service in 1962. Presently closed, the Park Service hopes to move the house to a site in St. Nicholas Park that more closely resembles its original environment.

Walk to the corner and turn left onto West 142nd Street

HH4 452-476 West 142nd Street

(George W. Spitzer, 1899-1900). Like the Beaux-Arts row around the corner (HH2), this limestone row exhibits the rich three-dimensional carving typical of the style. Unlike the Convent Avenue houses, however, these lack high stoops. They are examples of what is known as "American basement" houses, with the entrance nearly at street level and an interior stairway leading to the main level one story up. First introduced in New York in about 1880, these houses became increasingly popular in the 1890s. Note the narrow service entrances used by tradesmen and servants.

Stand in front of 458 West 142nd Street in order to best see all of the significant features of the church across the street.

HH5 Our Lady of Lourdes R.C. Church

467 West 142nd Street (O'Reilly Brothers, 1902-04). This designated landmark is unquestionably one of New York's most eccentric buildings, for it is an assemblage of pieces salvaged from three famous 19th-century structures. The street facade and much of the east side consist of sections of architect P.B. Wight's National Academy of Design of 1863-65; the stone pedestals that flank the front stair come from the "marble palace" of department store magnate A.T. Stewart; and the rear and one section of the side wall (visible down the alley) are James Renwick, Jr.'s original east end of St. Patrick's Cathedral. Architect Cornelius O'Reilly was fortunate that all three fragments became available in 1901-02 while planning

National Academy of Design, in the late 19th century; the source of much of the facade detail of Our Lady of Lourdes Church.

Rear elevation of Our Lady of Lourdes Church incorporating the original east end of St. Patrick's Cathedral, c. 1904.

Retrace your steps back to West 141st Street and Convent Avenue and turn left onto 141st Street. Cross Hamilton Terrace and continue east to St. Nicholas Avenue.

for the new church was underway, thus permitting the creation of this fascinating architectural pastiche.

HH6 St. Nicholas Avenue Presbyterian Church

Now St. James Presbyterian Church, 409 West 141st Street, northwest corner St. Nicholas Avenue (Ludlow & Valentine, 1904-05). As the population of Harlem increased, the Lenox Presbyterian Church outgrew its small buildings on West 139th Street (HC25) and erected this larger, Neo-Gothic structure on St. Nicholas Avenue (see photo, p.25). Less than a year after relocating, the congregation changed its name to reflect the new location. By the 1920s, the all white membership was in decline and in 1927 ownership was transferred to St. James, a black Presbyterian congregation. Organized in 1895, St. James originally held services on West 32nd Street, in the heart of the Tenderloin, then one of the most populous black sections of New York City. In 1903, the church moved to West 51st Street, also an African-American center, but in 1914 it became one of the first of the major churches to follow the African-American migration to Harlem. The congregation grew rapidly in Harlem, moving several times before settling into this building where it thrived under the leadership of Reverend Dr. William Lloyd Imes (HC19).

HH7 Harlem School of the Arts
645 St. Nicholas Avenue (Ulrich Franzen & Associates, 1974-79). The Harlem School of the Arts was established in 1963 at St. James Church by Dorothy Maynor (1911-1996) whose husband Shelby Rooks was rector. Maynor was one of the great operatic sopranos of the century, yet she was not able to sing on an opera stage since opera houses did not employ black artists. She did have a successful recital and recording career, making her New York debut at Town Hall in 1939 and her Carnegie Hall debut the next year. Maynor also sang at the inaugurations of presidents Truman and Eisenhower. Maynor was a pioneer who used her talent to blaze a trail for other African-American artists such as divas Leontyne Price, Marion Anderson, and Jessye Norman. In 1975, she became the first black member of the board of the Metropolitan Opera. Maynor founded the Harlem School of the Arts in order to offer poor children the opportunity to learn dance, music, and drama and "to make beauty in our community." She taught at the school and served as its executive director until 1979.

Turn left and walk a few yards north on St. Nicholas Avenue.

HH8 St. Nicholas Park
(Samuel Parsons, Jr., 1906-09). The steep, rocky outcropping extending south from 141st Street was designated a city park in the 1890s, with actual landscape design not beginning until 1906. Samuel Parsons, Jr., the city's chief landscape architect, preserved the rugged quality of the natural landscape while creating lawns at the base and walks that meander up the cliffs.

Return to West 141st Street. Look across the street to St. Nicholas Park.

HH9 City College of New York, Main Building
Now Shepard Hall (George B. Post, 1902-1907). Atop the cliff stands the campus of City College, focusing on the tower of Shepard Hall. City College (originally

St. Nicholas Park
prior to its transfor-
mation into a land-
scaped environment.
Note the advertise-
ments painted on the
rocks at right.

known as the Free Academy) was established in 1847 for
the education of men who graduated from public high
schools. The success of the school resulted in the 1897
purchase of this large uptown site. George B. Post's Collegiate Gothic buildings were constructed of gray Manhattan schist quarried on the site and ornamented with
contrasting white terra cotta. Collegiate Gothic was a
popular style on Ivy League campuses at the turn-of-the-
century. At City College, the style symbolized the fact
that the education received by New York's poor and
immigrant residents was every bit as good (if not better)

Main Building (now
Shepard Hall) at City
College rising above
St. Nicholas Park in
1908. Photo by
Wurts Brothers.

than that at the nation's most prestigious schools. Main Hall (renamed for board chairman Edward Morse Shepard), designed as a highly visible symbol of the college, contains academic facilities and a magnificent auditorium known as the Great Hall.

HH10 Hamilton Terrace

Hamilton Terrace exemplifies the preservation maxim that "the whole is greater than the sum of its parts," for no single building is outstanding in its own right, but together they create one of the city's loveliest streets. Hamilton Terrace was not part of the original Manhattan street grid, but was laid out by William De Forest as a private street, with plots along the blockfronts sold to speculative developers. The modest three-story rowhouses were erected between 1895 and 1902, with most construction occurring in 1897-99. Walk up the street and notice the variety of bricks—long, narrow Roman bricks, bricks of more typical dimensions, red bricks, yellow bricks, and beige bricks. Brownstone, limestone, and terra cotta add to the variety. Look for the details that enliven late 19th-century rowhouses; for example, carved stonework, iron cornices, and oak doors with flamboyant hardware.

HH11 Ivey Delph Apartments

19 Hamilton Terrace (Vertner W. Tandy, 1948-51). This Modern yellow brick apartment house with exposed concrete balconies was one of the last of buildings designed by Vertner Tandy, the first African-American architect registered in New York State. Tandy studied at the Tuskegee Institute and was graduated from the Cornell School of Architecture before moving to New York City where he lived for many years at 221 West 139th Street (HC22).

HH12 Mary Lou Williams Apartment

63 Hamilton Terrace (Neville & Bagge, 1911). Much of the success of the swinging Kansas City sound of Andy Kirk's band, Clouds of Joy, was due to the compositions and arrangements of pianist Mary Lou Williams (1910-

Return to Hamilton Terrace. At the corner, note the powerful massing of the apsidal east end of St. Luke's. Turn right.

Portrait of Mary Lou Williams. Photo by James J. Kriegsmann.

1981). Williams joined the band in 1928 and moved
with them to New York in 1936, becoming one of the
best-known performers of her day. Williams's contribu-
tion to the world of jazz was far reaching and many contemporary jazz musicians acknowledge the debt owed to
her artistry evident in such famous works as *Zodiac Suite*.

At the north end of
Hamilton Terrace
turn left onto West
144th Street.

HH13a 413-423 West 144th Street

(Thomas H. Dunn, 1898-1900) and **HH13b 418-426
West 144th Street** (Neville & Bagge, 1897). During the
late 19th century many styles of architecture were popular with the architects who specialized in the design of
New York's speculative rowhouses. The facade details on
middle-class rowhouses tended to echo, in a modest
way, the forms employed on the grand townhouses and
mansions designed by prestigious architects for wealthy
clients on the Upper East Side. The variety of designs is

evident on these two rows. To the north are houses faced with beige Roman brick ornamented with elaborate French Renaissance and Venetian Renaissance detail cast in terra cotta (look closely; the detail is quite wonderful). On the south side is a Beaux-Arts row capped by a French mansard roof and highlighted with an extensive array of cartouches (there are 45 on the 144th Street frontage!).

Walk to Convent Avenue and cross to the southwest corner of West 144th Street.

HH14 330-336 Convent Avenue

(Robert Dry, 1890-92). The design of these houses exemplifies the whimsy and originality of the best Queen Anne architecture. The dynamically massed facades incorporate rich textural and chromatic variations, evident despite the fact that several houses are painted. The varied materials include rough Manhattan schist (providing massive bases evident at Nos. 330 and 336), red sandstone, yellow brick, stained glass (intact at Nos. 330 and 332; note the address panels in the entry transoms), and red terra cotta (at No. 336). The employment of mock-Tudor half timbering, created with stone instead of traditional wood, adds a special character. The roofline is exceptionally exuberant, with its projecting towers, gables, dormers, and chimneys and its polygonal gray slate shingles.

Walk onto West 144th Street between Convent and Amsterdam avenues.

HH15a 452-466 West 144th Street

(William E. Mowbray, 1890) and **HH15b 453-467 West 144th Street** (William E. Mowbray, 1886-90). This block is a tour-de-force of rowhouse architecture. William Mowbray purchased both blockfronts from William De Forest, Jr., building the group on the north side of the street(see photo, p.90), before losing the southern property in a foreclosure action in 1889. Fortunately, de Forest, who actually built the row, retained Mowbray as architect. Although these houses are fantastically varied (in fact, no two are alike), innumerable materials are employed, and features are borrowed from many historic styles—Gothic, Tudor, Dutch, Romanesque, German and Italian Renaissance, Colonial, etc.—the block retains a cohesive quality. On the exterior, the houses are embellished with fascinating details.

453-459 West
144th Street, 1893.

Look for the date (1887) molded in terra cotta in the gables of Nos. 453 and 461, the monstrous creatures projecting from No. 465, and the heads at No. 467. Interior features also varied at each house. They were quite well appointed as this 1893 description of the parlor floor of No. 453 from *Scientific American* attests:

> The interior is planned with a view to combine convenience with elegance....The vestibule walls and ceiling are paneled, and the floor is laid in marble mosaic. The main hall is trimmed with antique oak, and the floor is laid in parquetry....The parlor is treated in ivory white, and the library in china white and gold. The parlor has a carved mantel, made from special design. The fireplace is built of brick, with facing of Mexican onyx and a hearth of tiles. The dining-room, spacious, is trimmed with antique oak. It has a paneled wainscoting and ceiling beams.

HH16 New York Public Library, Hamilton Grange Branch

503 West 145th Street (McKim, Mead & White, 1905-06). New York's burgeoning residential neighborhoods were not well-served by free libraries until Andrew Carnegie donated $5,000,000 to the New York Public Library for the construction of branches in 1901 (HC3, JT8). Charles McKim designed the finest branch libraries, including this landmark structure, an adaptation of the form of an Italian Renaissance palace. The quality of the design and detailing is extraordinary—note the rusticated limestone of the magnificently proportioned facade; the shield above the entrance with the seal of the city; the baby holding aloft an open book, carved onto the keystones above the ground-floor windows; and the spectacular wrought-iron railing.

Continue walking west to Amsterdam Avenue and turn right. Walk to West 145th Street. Turn left and walk a few yards west on West 145th Street.

HH17 Washington Heights Baptist Church

Now Convent Avenue Baptist Church (Lamb & Rich, 1897-99), 351 Convent Avenue, southeast corner West 145th Street. As with other churches in northern Manhattan, this Baptist church was erected by a downtown organization following its members as they moved into new residential neighborhoods. The Neo-Gothic building, faced in blocks of Georgia marble, was planned to seat approximately 1000 worshippers. The building was occupied by a white Baptist congregation until 1942 when it was sold to an African-American Baptist organization established in 1939. The congregation took the name Convent Avenue Baptist Church and has developed into one of the most prominent churches in the community.

Retrace your steps back to Amsterdam Avenue. Cross Amsterdam and continue east to Convent Avenue.

HH18 402-418 West 146th Street

(Neville & Bagge, 1893-94). Neville & Bagge, with offices on West 125th Street, was among the most prolific architectural firms in New York City between 1892 and 1930. The firm, best known for its apartment houses (HH25, JT10), designed many rowhouses early in its history, including this limestone row and those seen on 144th Street (HH13b). Textural contrasts between rough

Turn left, crossing West 145th Street and walking north. Turn right on West 146th Street.

and smooth stone enliven these facades. This is heightened by the quality of the stylized Byzantine carving seen at the base of the projecting oriels (at Nos. 410 and 412), at the windows, and on the post at the base of each stoop. For several decades, beginning in 1920, No. 402 was the home of the Bermuda Benevolent Association, a group established in 1898 as a social and relief organization for immigrants from Bermuda.

Walk to the corner of 146th Street and St. Nicholas Avenue, Turn left, and look across the street.

718-730 St. Nicholas Avenue,, 1893.

HH19 718-730 St. Nicholas Avenue

(A.B. Jennings, 1889-90). Early in his career, architect Arthur Bates Jennings designed a number of exuberant mansions and rowhouses, including this group of seven Romanesque Revival dwellings. Unfortunately, all of the houses have been shorn of their original stoops. The symmetrical row of rock-faced limestone houses has a lively roofline and facade details worth examining: Note, for example, the fierce dragons carved at the original entrances to the end houses and the stained-glass transoms, complete with address panel at Nos. 724 and 730. The side elevations of the towered end houses received light and air from 12 foot wide yards; such preservation

104

of valuable space in the middle of a block is extremely rare in New York City.

Walk a few feet north on St. Nicholas Avenue.

729-731 St. Nicholas Avenue photographed shortly after their completion in 1886.

HH20 729-731 St. Nicholas Avenue

(Thomas Minot Clark, 1885-86). One of the wonderful aspects of walking around New York City is coming unexpectedly upon buildings of such oddity that you are forced to stop for a closer examination. Despite the loss of entry stoops, these houses are such a pair. The fact that Thomas Minot Clark was far better trained than most rowhouse designers, having worked as an assistant to the great American architect Henry Hobson Richardson, is evident in the complexity of the design. These are perhaps the only rowhouses in the city faced primarily with Manhattan schist. The roughness of the stone is relieved by yellow terra-cotta, bricks molded with projecting bosses, and wooden shingles.

HH21 Ralph Ellison Apartment

749 St. Nicholas Avenue (Edward E. Ashley, 1905-06). Novelist and essayist Ralph Ellison (1914-1994) wrote the novel *Invisible Man* while living in an apartment in this building. *Invisible Man*, which won the National Book Award in 1952, is a metaphoric exploration of the African-American experience from slavery to the 20th century. Ellison came to Harlem in the late 1930s. Through poet Langston Hughes (OS10) he met Richard

Continue north, crossing West 147th Street.

Wright, author of *Black Boy*, who had a profound influence on him. Wright encouraged Ellison to read great literature and consider writing as a career. Ellison received the nation's highest civilian award, the Medal of Freedom, in 1976.

Return to West 147th Street and turn right.

HH22 West 147th Street between St. Nicholas and Convent Avenues.

The 36 rowhouses that line this street were erected between 1890 and 1900, the peak years of residential development on the Bradhurst property. The most eye-catching of the rows is that at Nos. 401-409 designed in 1895 by an especially obscure architect, Frederick P. Dinkelberg. Most striking are the marvelous stepped stoop walls with their sinuous wrought ironwork. On the south side, almost all of the houses are faced with limestone. Limestone, transported by railroad from quarries in Indiana, became widely popular in the 1890s as the taste waned for the earth-toned brick and stone rowhouses of the 1880s, seen on Convent Avenue and on 144th Street (HH14-15). Many of the houses display the stylized Byzantine carving typical of the Romanesque Revival style. The houses at Nos. 412-430 and at the northeast corner of Convent Avenue are ornamented with Byzantine carving of the highest quality. The beautiful stylized vines and basketweaves were created by anonymous immigrant stone carvers using both machine and hand tools.

Continue to the corner of Convent Avenue.

HH23 400 Convent Avenue

Northwest corner West 147th Street (Frank M. Wright, 1910). By the early years of the 20th century, rowhouse construction in Hamilton Heights had virtually ceased and middle-class apartment houses were erected in increasing numbers. This building, designed in a medieval-inspired style, perhaps inspired by the nearby presence of City College, is one of the handsomest in the neighborhood. The sizable courtyards were required by a 1901 law that sought to assure that adequate light and air would reach every room in each of the 35 apartments.

Turn right onto
Convent Avenue
and walk to 148th
Street.

400 Convent Avenue
in c.1940.

HH24 408-418 and 420-430 Convent Avenue

Southwest and northwest corners West 148th Street
(John Hauser, 1896 and 1897). Convent Avenue originally ran only as far north as 145th Street, but in 1894 it
was cut through to 152nd Street and St. Nicholas
Avenue. This caused the demolition of Pinehurst, the
Bradhurst's estate house which had become the Mount
St. Vincent Hotel, and which stood in the middle of the
juncture of Convent Avenue and 148th Street (see photo,
p. 89). Soon after the avenue was opened, rowhouses
appeared, including these two groups of Romanesque
Revival dwellings designed by the prolific local Harlem
architect John Hauser (HC19).

Continue north.

The Rev. Adam Clayton Powell, Sr. preaching.

HH25 Emsworth Hall and the Adam Clayton Powell, Sr. Apartment

Now Garrison Apartments, 435 Convent Avenue, southeast corner West 149th Street (Neville & Bagge, 1909-10). An unusual apartment building with a massive granite base, this was, for many years, the home of the dynamic Adam Clayton Powell, Sr. (1865-1953). Powell came to New York in 1908 when he was called to the ministry of Abyssinian Baptist Church (HC30), then located on West 40th Street. He was quickly recognized as a national leader for the black community. Powell was a supporter of the "On to Harlem" movement. He moved to Harlem himself and then persuaded his congregation to follow. Throughout his life, Powell was a vocal advocate of self-help through education and sound economic ventures.

Walk to the corner of 149th Street.

Presentation drawing for the Church of the Crucifixion, 1965.

HH26 Episcopal Church of the Crucifixion

459 West 149th Street, northwest corner Convent Avenue (Costas Machlouzarides, 1965-67). Undoubtedly the most unusual stop on this tour, the Church of the Crucifixion is the only church in New York City inspired by Le Corbusier's chapel at Ronchamp in France. While not as dynamic as Corbu's masterpiece, the church is quite an expressive essay in the use of reinforced concrete. The sweeping roof floats above clerestory windows and is cantilevered over a series of curved masses, each outlining a specific interior feature—the altar facing Convent Avenue, and the baptistery, a shrine, and a chapel along 149th Street. This Episcopal church with a black congregation was organized in 1916, moving into an older church on this corner in 1938; fire destroyed that building in 1963 and the new structure was erected on the old foundations.

HH27a 8 St. Nicholas Place

Southeast corner West 150th Street (Richard Rosenstock, 1885-86) and **HH27b Jacob P. Baiter House,** 6 St. Nicholas Place (Theodore G. Stein, 1893-95), both now the Dawn Hotel. St. Nicholas Place became a popular spot for picturesque suburban villas in the 1880s. Although it has been altered, the corner house retains much of the Queen Anne detail common on these freestanding dwellings. Still evident are the complex roof slopes, ornamental pressed-metal details, tall chimney, and a winged monster atop the central gable. The house to the right, at No. 6, erected for yeast manufacturer Jacob P.

Turn right on West 149th Street. Walk to St. Nicholas Avenue. Cross 149th Street and then cross St. Nicholas Avenue, stopping at the triangular park.

The suburban quality of St. Nicholas Place is evident in this photograph of c.1890 with 8 St. Nicholas Place at right and the James Bailey House in the center.

Baiter, is a more subdued, Renaissance-inspired dwelling of yellow Roman brick with terra-cotta trim. Nos. 6 and 8 were connected in about 1912 when they were converted into a psychiatric sanitorium; the buildings later served as Community Hospital before becoming a hotel.

Walk to the southwest corner of St. Nicholas Place and West 150th Street.

James Bailey House, 1890.

HH28   James A. and Ruth Bailey Residence

Now M. Marshall Blake Funeral Home, 10 St. Nicholas Place, northeast corner West 150th Street (Samuel B. Reed, 1886-88). How appropriate that James A. Bailey, "the king of circus men," would build such a flamboyant home for his family. Bailey, one of the world's great showmen, established his own circus in 1872 before forming a partnership with his competitor Phineas T. Barnum in 1881. The freestanding house is a picturesque limestone structure with an exciting silhouette of Flemish-inspired gables, a large tower, and crocketed corner towerlettes reminiscent of a medieval castle. The house contains one of the most extensive installations of Belcher mosaic glass. Patented in 1884 by Henry F. Belcher, this glass was mass produced at a factory in Irvington, New Jersey and for a brief period was quite popular on New York City dwellings. The panels were made by arranging small glass "tesserae" on a flat surface, then binding them together with molten metal poured between the shards. Abstract panels, often highlighted with small jewels, were the most common, but complex scenic windows were also produced. At the Bailey House, Belcher glass survives on all facades.

After examining the detail on the Bailey House and noting the two adjacent suburban villas, now heavily altered, at 14 and 16 St. Nicholas Place (William M. Grinnell, 1883), turn onto 150th Street. Walk along the side of the Bailey house, noting the conservatory at the rear. Proceed to Edgecombe Avenue.

Rear yards of St. Nicholas Place houses sloping down to Edgecombe Avenue, c. 1889.

HH29 Edgecombe Avenue and Colonial Park

Now Jackie Robinson Park (Samuel Parsons, Jr., 1907-08). This street runs along the edge of a "combe," a British word meaning deep valley. Land along the cliff was acquired by the city in 1899. The park that was opened to the public in 1908 was originally known as Colonial Park and is a northern extension of St. Nicholas Park (HH8). The park was renamed for the great baseball player Jackie Robinson in 1978. When Branch Rickey signed Robinson to play for the Brooklyn Dodger's farm team in Montreal on October 23, 1945 he effectively ended segregation in the sport. Two years later, Robinson became the first black major league player when he debuted with the Dodgers.

HH30 Nicholas and Agnes Benziger House

345 Edgecombe Avenue, northwest corner West 150th Street (Schickel & Co., 1890-91). Nicholas Benziger, a publisher of Catholic books, was one of a number of wealthy people who erected large homes in this area to take advantage of the views to the east towards the Bronx and the Long Island Sound. To design his house, Benziger, who was a German-speaking Swiss immigrant, hired German emigré architect William Schickel. Both Benziger and Schickel were part of a social circle of wealthy and successful New York Catholics. This simple well-proportioned house faced in a beautifully-colored brick is typical of Schickel's work during the 1890s.

Look north up this long block or walk north to the tall building at the corner of West 155th Street.

HH31 409 Edgecombe Avenue

(Schwartz & Gross, 1916-17). This handsome, 12-story, Renaissance-inspired apartment house, originally known as the Colonial Parkway Apartments, was the most prestigious address in Sugar Hill from the 1930s through the 1950s, attracting so many members of the nation's black elite that in 1947 *Ebony* commented that "legend, only slightly exaggerated, says bombing 409 would wipe out Negro leadership for next 20 years." Among those who called 409 home during its heyday were singer Julius Bledsoe who originated the role of Joe in *Show Boat* in 1927 and was the first to sing the renowned *Ole Man River*; poet and novelist William Braithwaite; Eunice Carter, one of the first African-American woman judges in New York State; May Chinn, a pioneering African-American woman physician; the great artist and mural painter

112

Aaron Douglas; the renowned scholar, writer, and soci-
ologist W.E.B. DuBois who was a founder of the NAACP
and the editor of *Crisis*, one of the most influential
African-American magazines of the 20th century; Thur-
good Marshall, the first African-American U.S. Supreme
Court justice; Walter White, chief executive of the
NAACP whose apartment was known as "The White
House of Harlem"; and Roy Wilkens who succeeded
White as the head of the NAACP.

*409 Edgecombe
Avenue shortly after
its completion.*

Jumel Terrace Tour

Introduction

This short walk examines the small residential enclave adjacent to the Morris-Jumel Mansion. Although an extremely compact area, with only a few buildings, the history of this area vividly exemplifies the waves of residential development that transformed lower Washington Heights from a rural retreat to an urban neighborhood. During the Colonial era, the high elevations overlooking the Harlem and Hudson rivers, swept by cooling breezes and far from the turmoil of the crowded city to the south, attracted wealthy families who laid out country estates. Lieutenant Colonel Roger Morris and his wife Mary Philipse Morris erected their magnificent home, known as Mount Morris, in 1765. It was here that George Washington established his headquarters in 1776 during the Revolutionary War Battle of Washington Heights. In 1810, the property was purchased by Stephen and Eliza Jumel. It was not until 1882 that the Jumel's heirs divided the property into 1058 city lots and sold them at auction. Immediately following the sale,

Madame Jumel's cypress trees and the rear elevations of 418-428 West 160th Street, c.1895.

Sylvan Terrace was lined with small wooden houses, a reflection of the early urbanization of Washington Heights, as inexpensive wooden dwellings were erected throughout the neighborhood. Between 1891 and 1903, 31 rowhouses appeared in the area. Such rowhouse development was very limited in this section of Washington Heights since mass transit connections to Lower Manhattan were poor. The closest station on the elevated railroad was inconveniently located at Eighth Avenue and 155th Street—a substantial hike along a steep slope.

Washington Heights was destined to become a neighborhood, not of middle-class rowhouses, but of apartment buildings. As mass transit improved, especially with the opening of the IRT subway on Broadway in 1904, hundreds of apartment houses were erected. Six-story elevator buildings, such as the Jumel Terrace on 160th Street, planned for modest middle-class families, typify the new development. A few grander structures, including 555 Edgecombe Avenue, were built for more affluent families. The early occupants of the new housing were a multi-ethnic group that was entirely white. By the 1930s, the racial character of the neighborhood was changing as many African-Americans moved into the area.

The Jumel Terrace Historic District was designated by the New York City Landmarks Preservation Commission in 1970 and since that time many houses have been restored, notably the wooden buildings on Sylvan Terrace. Today, the Jumel Terrace area remains one of the most pleasant enclaves in northern Manhattan.

Tour

Begin: West 162nd Street just east of St. Nicholas Avenue.

JT1 425-439 and 441-451 West 162nd Street

(Walter H.C. Hornum, 1894-95 and 1895). The rowhouses on both sides of West 162nd Street create an exceptionally well-preserved example of a late 19th-century residential streetscape. The importance of the stoop is especially evident on the north side, where all of the high stoops are extant, visually anchoring each house to the sidewalk. The row to the west has stoops with stone walls, while the stoops to the east support fine iron railings. The houses are faced with either white limestone or brown sandstone, with simple Renaissance-inspired detail. Note the original multi-paneled oak entrance doors and the glass storm doors. By 1900, all but one house was owner-occupied, with the families of businessmen, a watch importer, a realtor, a fireman, and a clerk. Most had at least one servant and several had two or three.

JT2   440-444 West 162nd Street

(Neville & Bagge, 1902-03). This trio of Beaux-Arts rowhouses is the most exuberant in the district, with its boldly-carved cartouches, huge brackets hung with garlands, and projecting oriel windows. Thomas Neville and George Bagge began their careers as rowhouse designers (HH13b, HH18), but their firm went on to become one of the city's most prolific designers of apartment houses (HH25, JT10).

Walk east and cross Jumel Terrace. Stand on the southeast corner.

JT3   Jumel Terrace

A surprisingly large amount of 19th-century paving material survives in New York. On Jumel Terrace you can see two of the most popular materials employed on the city's streets. The sidewalks are bluestone, a type of sandstone that was the most popular sidewalk material in New York's older residential neighborhoods. The streets are paved in Belgian blocks. These are granite blocks quarried in New England that resemble the blocks used to pave the plazas of Belgian cities. These blocks are often incorrectly referred to as cobblestones (cobblestones are small stones washed smooth by water). Also note the retaining wall on Roger Morris Park which is constructed from locally-quarried Manhattan schist.

JT4   430-438 West 162nd Street and 10-18 Jumel Terrace

(Henri Fouchaux, 1896-97). Although the five houses at 430-438 West 162nd Street and the five on Jumel Terrace have different designs they were built as a single unit. Each group is a copy of one of the earlier houses designed by Walter Hornum on the north side of 162nd Street: Nos. 430-438 are almost identical to Nos. 441-451 and the Jumel Terrace houses are limestone versions of the brownstone houses at Nos. 425-439. This brings up the interesting issue of who exactly was responsible for the design of speculative rowhouses. Men such as Hornum and Fouchaux probably had very little formal architectural training. The choices made by the builders and the work undertaken by the anonymous stone carvers probably had as much to do with the aesthetics of the rowhouse facades as the designs of the architects who specialized in the creation of speculative rowhouses.

Walk down Jumel Terrace.

JT5 Paul Robeson House

16 Jumel Terrace (Henri Fouchaux, 1896-97). Paul Robeson (1898-1976), intellectual, actor, athlete, political activist, and world-renowned singer was one of the best known African-Americans in the United States between the 1920s and 1950s. His voice was almost as well recognized as that of Franklin Roosevelt as it sang out across the radio waves "like a vibrant tide," as he crisscrossed the country on concert tours, or appeared in movies such as *Show Boat*. Yet, his outspoken views on racism in America and his support for socialism branded him a traitor. In the 1950s, he was a target of both the FBI and the House Un-American Activities Committee which tried to prevent his traveling abroad, speaking publicly, or making a living. Robeson lived briefly at 555 Edgecombe Avenue (JT11) beginning in 1939. He and his wife Eslanda Cardozo Goode Robeson, known as Essie (an anthropologist, author, and Pan-Africanist) moved into this house in the 1950s. Paul Robeson lived here intermittently until 1967.

Paul Robeson at a recording session, 1933.

JT6 Mount Morris, The Morris-Jumel Mansion

(1764; remodeling, c.1810). In 1764, Roger Morris, a Lieutenant Colonel in the British army, and his wife Mary Philipse purchased 115 acres in northern Manhattan and erected this elegant country house. Typifying Georgian design, the house is symmetrical, with a central

Turn left into Roger Morris Park and walk to the lawn in front of the Morris-Jumel Mansion.

The Morris-Jumel mansion in the mid 19th century.

entrance, quoins marking each end of the facade, and a hip roof. The double-height portico is exceptional for its early date and the octagonal room at the rear is thought to be the first in America. The high elevation provided the house with panoramic views of the New Jersey Palisades, the Long Island Sound, and the growing city of New York to the south. Morris was a loyalist and returned to England in 1775 when the Revolutionary War began. From September 14 to October 18, 1776 this was the headquarters of General George Washington who used the elevated site to supervise the retreat of his troops from Manhattan. Following the war, the estate was confiscated and sold, serving as a roadhouse and a stop for the Albany stage.

After passing through several hands, the estate was purchased in 1810 by wealthy French wine and brandy importer Stephen Jumel and his wife Eliza. The Jumels modernized the house, adding, for example, the Federal style fanlit entrance. Eliza Jumel died in 1865, but sixteen years of litigation tied up the property. Fortunately, when the estate was auctioned in 1882, Jumel's son-in-law, Nelson Chase, bought the house and its immediate surroundings. As early as 1887, when Chase sold the property, concerned citizens were suggesting that it should become a museum. However, the future of the property remained uncertain until the city's purchase in 1903 and the creation of Roger Morris Park. Even then, the preservation of the house was far from assured, as two women's patriotic organizations—the Daughters of the American Revolution (DAR) and the Colonial Dames—fought bitterly over who should organized the historic house museum. Eventually, the city decided to retain ownership of the house, but allow the DAR to run the property. In 1992, the city completed a restoration of the exterior, by Jan Hird Pokorny, Architects.

JT7 Sylvan Terrace

Exit the park and walk straight ahead onto Sylvan Terrace.

(Gilbert Robinson, Jr., 1882-83). Large numbers of small wooden dwellings were erected in lower Washington Heights in the post-Civil War period. The twenty Sylvan Terrace houses are not only the largest unified development, but are among the few surviving. The street was laid out as a private thoroughfare, generally following the line of the carriage drive leading from St. Nicholas Avenue to Mount Morris House. The detail on the facades provides evidence of the mechanization of wood carving, for the original entrance hoods with their perforated brackets and pendants, the cornices supported by ornate brackets, the high stoops with their turned balusters and newel posts, the double doors, and the window enframements with their "cupid's bow" sills were all mass produced on wooden lathes, saws, and other machines. Inside, the houses originally had seven small rooms on the upper two floors; the cellar was unfinished. Running water was provided, but toilets were in the yards.

Few of the houses were owner-occupied in the 19th or early 20th centuries. Most were held as investments by people who lived elsewhere. The houses were occupied primarily by civil servants and laborers. In 1900 the occupations of residents included policeman, feed dealer, fireman, harness maker, detective, painter, cooper, telephone operator, music teacher, and dressmaker. The sons and daughters of residents were often employed at relatively young ages. Most residents were American born, but there were also a substantial number of Irish and a few people from Germany, England, and Scotland. Several residents kept boarders, but no one on the street had income to support a live-in servant.

Over the years, all of the houses were heavily altered,

Sylvan Terrace looking west, c.1900.

with facade details removed and the clapboards covered or replaced with a myriad of residing materials. In 1977, the Landmarks Preservation Commission, with funding provided by the federal government, began a facade restoration project. Owners could have their facades restored free and all except the owner of No. 16 took advantage of this offer.

Continue to the end of Sylvan Terrace. Walk down the steps and turn left.

JT8 New York Public Library, Washington Heights Branch

1000 St. Nicholas Avenue, northeast corner West 160th Street (Carrère & Hastings, 1912-14). This library is the successor to the Washington Heights Free Library, a privately-funded library opened to the public in 1883. It is one of the 67 public libraries erected in New York City with money donated by Andrew Carnegie. The simple Renaissance-inspired brick building was designed by the firm responsible for the main library on Fifth Avenue and 42nd Street and for thirteen other branch libraries

Turn left onto West 160th Street.

.

JT9 418-430 West 160th Street

(418: Walgrove & Israels, 1890-91; 420-430: Richard R.

New York Public Library, *Washington Heights Branch* in 1925.

Davis, 1891-92). These seven brick and sandstone houses are the earliest masonry rowhouses in the district. Close examination reveals the talents of the anonymous stone carvers, most of whom were immigrants, largely Italian, but also German and Greek, working in commercial stone yards or, in some cases, right at the building site. Note the fantastical birds and grimacing heads that enliven many of the facades and the pineapple (symbol of hospitality) carved above the entrance of No. 420.

JT10 Jumel Terrace Apartments

425 West 160th Street (Neville & Bagge, 1909). Six years after designing the trio of rowhouses on West 162nd Street (JT2), Neville & Bagge designed this apartment building, one of many that rose in southern Washington Heights just before and after 1910. The building's developer was architect Thomas P. Neville. This is a handsome middle-class structure with beige brick (now

quite dirty), a limestone base, ornate entrance, and terra-cotta trim. Note the iron grille at the front doors and the fire escapes on Jumel Terrace that resemble Parisian balconies. Unfortunately, the building has lost its cornice.

Continue walking east to the corner of Edgecombe Avenue.

JT11 555 Edgecombe Avenue

Southwest corner West 160th Street (Schwartz & Gross, 1914-16). Although outside the boundaries of the Jumel Terrace Historic District, this apartment house was designated as an individual landmark in 1993 in recognition of its importance as home to many prominent African-Americans. Originally known as the Roger Morris, the apartments in this building were rented to white tenants. In 1939, leases were not renewed and apartments were rented to African-Americans. Most were typical middle-class families, but among those who soon moved in were the renowned singer, actor, and political activist Paul Robeson (JT5); the great jazz artist Count Basie; social psychologist Kenneth Clark; and actor/producer Canada Lee.

555 Edgecombe Avenue in 1948.

122

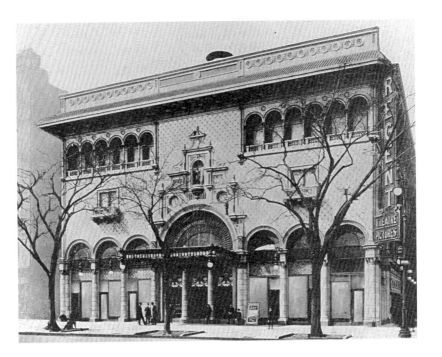

Other Sites

Regent Theater in 1914.

OS1 Regent Theater

Now First Corinthian Baptist Church, 1906-1916 Adam
Clayton Powell, Jr., southwest corner West 116th Street
(Thomas Lamb, 1912-13). The Regent was one of the
earliest movie palaces in America and one of the major
buildings of Thomas Lamb, an architect who specialized
in this type of fantasy architecture. The extraordinary
Italian Renaissance-inspired facade is covered in richly-
colored terra cotta. The building was saved when it was
purchased by the First Corinthian Baptist Church in
1964.

Note: Sites
arranged from
south to north.

OS2 Graham Court Apartments

1927 Adam Clayton Powell, Jr. Boulevard between West
116th and 117th Streets (Clinton & Russell, 1899-
1901). The Italian Renaissance style Graham Court,
Harlem's grandest apartment house, was built by

William Waldorf Astor with a landscaped courtyard entered through an arch that is clad in Guastavino tile.

OS3 Minton's Playhouse
206-210 West 118th Street. Located on the ground floor of the Cecil Hotel, Minton's was the jazz club that nurtured the bebop revolution in the 1940s. After playing more traditional jazz and dance-band favorites at Harlem's clubs, musicians such as Kenny Clarke, Thelonius Monk, Dizzie Gillespie, and Charlie Parker would arrive for late-night improvisational jam sessions. The new owners of the Cecil hope to revive the famous club.

OS4 St. Thomas the Apostle R.C. Church
260 West 118th Street (Thomas H. Poole & Co., 1904-07). A strikingly eccentric Neo-Gothic church of gold Roman brick and spectacular beige terra cotta. The interior is as complex as the facade.

125th Street looking west with the *Apollo* Theatre at the right, c.1940s.

125th Street (OS5-OS9)

As Harlem developed, 125th Street became the community's great commercial thoroughfare, lined with small shops, large department stores, theaters, banks, and

hotels. With the increase in Harlem's black population, many of these establishments refused to hire African-Americans or had segregated admission policies. Only after political action on the part of residents did 125th Street become "Main Street" for black Harlem.

Performers at the Apollo Theater, 1939.

Among the major buildings on 125th Street are:

OS5 Apollo Theater

253 West 125th Street (George Keister, 1913-14). Frank Schiffman and Leo Brecher, former owners of Harlem's popular Lafayette Theater, purchased Hurtig & Seamon's New Theater, a former burlesque house, in 1934 and renamed it the Apollo. They proceeded to create what would be one of the most significant and long lasting showcases for African-American talent in the country. Most of America's successful black entertainers have played the Apollo and it continues to serve as a vital cultural venue in Harlem.

OS6 Hotel Theresa

2082-2096 Adam Clayton Powell, Jr. Boulevard, south-

The Hotel Theresa on Seventh Avenue and 125th Street in 1953. Photo by Austin Hansen.

west corner West 125th Street (George & Edward Blum, 1912-13). The Theresa is a major design by George & Edward Blum, displaying this firm's distinctive use of shallow, overlapping, geometric patterns of white terracotta ornament. The hotel was only desegregated in 1940, after which it became known as "the Waldorf of Harlem." It was a local social center, frequented by many black celebrities. The first black manager of the Theresa was William Harmon Brown. This was the childhood home of his son, Ron Brown, who later became chairman of the Democratic Party and was President Bill Clinton's Secretary of Commerce at the time of his tragic death in an airplane crash. The Theresa gained national notoriety in 1960 when Fidel Castro stayed here on a visit to the United Nations, hosting, among others, Russian premier Nikita Khrushchev. The hotel also housed offices of important community groups, including A. Phillip Randolph's March on Washington Movement and Malcolm X's Organization of Afro-American Unity. The hotel was converted to an office building in 1970.

The Citizens' League For Fair Play

requests all self-respecting people of Harlem to

Refuse to Trade with
L. M. BLUMSTEIN
230 West 125th Street

¶ This firm, acknowledging its large propor-
tion of Negro business, has refused to employ
Negro Clerks.

Stay out of Blumstein's!
Refuse to buy there !

This Campaign is endorsed and receiving cooperation from the following churches and organizations:

Abyssinian Baptist
Beulah Wesleyan Meth.
Ephesus Seventh Day
   Adventists
Good Samaritan
   Independent Episcopal
Grace Gospel
Hubert Harrison
   Memorial
Mother A.M.E. Zion
Mt. Calvary M.E.
Mt. Olivet Baptist
Refuge Church of God
Shiloh Baptist
St. Martin's Episcopal
St. Mathew's Baptist
St. James Presbyterian
St. Paul's Baptist
Transfiguration Lutheran
United Seventh Day
   Adventists
Union Baptist
African Patriotic League
African Vanguard
Afro-American Voters'
   Coalition
Aster Social and Literary
   Club
Dunbar Literary Club

Business and Professional
   Men's Association
Col. Young Memorial
   Foundation
Central Harlem Medical
   Association
Cosmopolitan Social and
   Tennis Club
Day Worker's League
Dumont Literary Club
Eureka Lodge of
   Oddfellows
Excelsior Lodge, No. 4,
   Preston Univ
Excelsior Literary Club
Garvey Club of N. Y., Inc.
Junior Fellowship,
   St. Philip's
Harlem Women's Ass'n
Keystone Lodge, I.U.O.M.
Ladies & African
   Patriotic League
Manhattan Civic Center
Mills Citizens Voters
   League
New York Age
N. Y. Chapter of Nat.
   Ass'n for College
   Women

N. Y. Chapter, U. N. I. A.
Neptune Lodge Elks.
Negro Youth Progressive
   Ass'n
New York News
Harlem Com. Center
Political Voters
Premier Literary Circle
Progressive Negro Youth
   of America
Progressive Political Ass'n
Charles Romney Fusion
   Rep. Club, 11th A.D.
J. A. Rogers Historical
   Research Society
The Sentinels
Students' Literary Ass'n
   St. Mark's Epis. Church
The Intense Social Club
Undergraduate Chapter of
   Phi Beta Sigma
United Negro Progressive
   Ass'n
Unity Democratic Club
Unique Musical Club
Unison Social Club
Yoruba Literary Club
Young West Indian
   Congress

Don't fail to be in line in the Grand Parade and Demonstration on Saturday, July 28th. All persons are requested to form on 138th Street between Lenox and Seventh Avenues at 10 o'clock.

Broadside supporting
boycott of
Blumstein's.

OS7 Blumstein's

230 West 125th Street (Robert D. Kohn and Charles But-
ler, 1921-23). Blumstein's, once the largest department
store in Harlem, was established by German-immigrant
Louis Blumstein in 1898. Like many white-owned stores
in Harlem, Blumstein's refused to hire black workers for
anything but menial positions. In 1934, Blumstein's was
chosen as a target for a "Don't Buy Where You Can't
Work" boycott. The victory in integrating Blumstein's

helped break down the barriers of segregation in employment in urban areas of the North and demonstrated the power of joint effort on the part of people seeking equal rights. Blumstein's later became the first store with a black Santa and the first to use black mannequins.

OS8 Koch's Department Store
132-140 West 125th Street (William H. Hume; 1890; two additional stories, 1893). The Koch name is still emblazoned on the pediment of this building, once one of the major department stores of New York City.

OS9 Mount Morris Bank
81-85 East 125th Street, northwest corner Park Avenue (Lamb & Rich, 1883-84; enlarged 1889-90). A masterful Queen Anne structure that originally housed a bank with apartments above. The facades are enlivened with superb terra-cotta decoration. Unfortunately this city owned building is vacant and deteriorating. Although the Landmarks Conservancy sponsored an engineering design for its stabilization and re-roofing, municipal budget cutbacks have prevented work from proceeding. Sadly a fire seriously damaged the vacant building in 1997 and the two upper stories had to be removed.

OS10 Langston Hughes Apartment
20 East 127th Street (Alexander Wilson, 1869). The work of James Langston Hughes (1902-1967), one of the greatest American poets and writers of prose, vividly characterizes the hopes, dreams, and lives of African-Americans. The great body of his work also documents the urban folk-life of black Americans, incorporating jazz, blues, and folk speech. Hughes was one of the most prolific Harlem Renaissance writers and works such as *Montage of a Dream Deferred* describe life in Harlem. Hughes lived on the top floor of this rowhouse from 1947 until his death.

OS11 Astor Row

8-62 West 130th Street (Charles Buek, 1880-83). Astor
Row is one of Harlem's earliest major residential construction projects. Built on land owned by William
Astor, the 28 simple brick houses are graced with an
extraordinary series of wooden porches. In 1992, the
New York Landmarks Conservancy, in association with
the Landmarks Preservation Commission and the
Abyssinian Development Corporation began an ongoing
project to reverse serious deterioration and restore these
extraordinary houses.

*West 130th Street
looking east from
Lenox Avenue with
Astor Row at right,
c.late 1940s.*

OS12 Dunbar Apartments

2588 Adam Clayton Powell, Jr. Boulevard (Andrew J.
Thomas, 1926-28). Encompassing an entire block
between 149th and 150th streets, the Dunbar, named for
the great black poet Paul Laurence Dunbar, was erected
by John D. Rockefeller, Jr. as a non-profit cooperative for
African-Americans. Set around a landscaped garden and
playground, the walk-up buildings attracted many
prominent residents including arctic explorer Matthew
Henson, singer and political activist Paul Robeson (JT5),
sociologist and writer W.E.B. DuBois, union organizer A.
Philip Randolph (HC17), and dancer Bill "Bojangles"
Robinson.

Sculptor Heinz War-
necke's "Mother and
Child" at Harlem
River House, 1937.

OS13 Harlem River Houses

MacCombs Place, Harlem River, 151st to 153rd Streets
(Archibald Manning Brown, chief architect, 1936-37).
Harlem River Houses was a pioneering federally-funded
housing project consisting of a complex of low-rise
buildings with 574 apartments set around generous
landscaped open space (see photo, p.16). It was planned
exclusively for African-American tenants and included
among its designers black architect John Louis Wilson.
The courtyard arches are embellished with relief sculp-
tures by Heinz Warnecke. Harlem River Houses remains
one of New York's finest public housing complexes.

130

OS14 Duke Ellington Apartment

935 St. Nicholas Avenue (Gronenburg & Leuchtag, 1915-16). Duke Ellington (1899-1974), one of America's greatest composers and musicians lived in apartment 4A of this Sugar Hill building between 1939 and 1961. Born in Washington, D.C., Edward Kennedy Ellington arrived in Harlem in 1923 and worked as a ragtime piano player. In 1923 he took over the band at the Cotton Club, beginning a twelve year association with that famous night spot. Ellington's impeccable style and suave appearance were trademarks and his musical compositions not only reflected a commitment to preserving black culture, but also changed American music. Among his most famous compositions are *Black and Tan Fantasy* (1927), *Mood Indigo* (1931), *Creole Rhapsody* (1931), and *It Don't Mean a Thing If It Ain't Got That Swing* (1932).

Duke Ellington and his band in 1943.

Local Resources

For information on how you can assist in the preservation of Harlem's buildings, or more information about local preservation efforts, you can contact the following organizations:

Hamilton Heights Homeowners Association
P.O. Box 565, Hamilton Grange Station
New York, N.Y. 10031
212-281-4442

Historic Districts Council
232 East 11th Street, New York, N.Y. 10003
212-614-9107

Mount Morris Park Community
    Improvement Association
74 West 124th Street, New York, N.Y. 10027
212-369-4241

New York City Landmarks Preservation Commission
100 Old Slip, New York, N.Y. 10005
212-487-6700

New York Landmarks Conservancy
141 Fifth Avenue, New York, N.Y. 10010
212-995-5260

Cultural Institutions
Local cultural institutions of interest include the following:

The Studio Museum in Harlem
144 West 125th Street, between Lenox and Seventh Avenues. A noteworthy cultural institution, the museum features various important exhibitions of African-American art (212-864-4500).

The Dance Theater of Harlem
466 West 152nd Street. Housed in a complex of modern architecture and historic buildings, the theater is a dynamic multicultural institution comprised of students and dancers from around the world (212-690-2800).

Selected Bibliography

Anderson, Jervis, *This Was Harlem: A Cultural Portrait 1900-1950* NY: Farrar Straus Giroux, 1981.

Dolkart, Andrew S., *Guide to New York City Landmarks,* NY: John Wiley & Sons, 1998.

Floyd, Samuel A., Jr., *Black Music in the Harlem Renaissance: A Collection of Essays* Knoxville: University of Tennessee Press, 1993.

Green, Charles and Basil Wilson, *The Struggle for Black Empowerment in New York City: Beyond the Politics of Pigmentation* NY: Praeger, 1989.

Greenberg, Cheryl Lynn, *Or Does It Explode: Black Harlem in the Depression* NY: Oxford University Press, 1991.

Johnson, James Weldon, *Black Manhattan* NY: Knopf, 1930.

Lewis, David Levering, *When Harlem was In Vogue* NY: Knopf, 1979.

McKay, Claude, *Harlem: Negro Metropolis* NY: E.P. Dutton & Co., 1940.

New York City Landmarks Preservation Commission, *Hamilton Heights Historic District Designation Report* (1974), *Jumel Terrace Historic District Designation Report* (1970), *Mount Morris Historic District Designation Report* (1971), *St. Nicholas Historic District Designation Report* (1967).

Osofsky, Gilbert, *Harlem: The Making of a Ghetto...Negro New York, 1890-1930* NY: Harper & Row, 1971.

Riker, James, *Revised History of Harlem* NY: New Harlem Publishing Co., 1904.

Scheiner, Seth M., *Negro Mecca: A History of the Negro in New York City, 1865-1920* NY: New York University Press, 1965.

Schoener, Allon, ed. *Harlem on My Mind* NY: Random House, 1968.

Watson, Steven, *The Harlem Renaissance: Hub of African-American Culture, 1920-1930* NY: Pantheon, 1995.

Willensky, Elliot and Norval White, *AIA Guide to New York City*, San Diego; Harcourt Brace Jovanovich, 1988.

Illustration Sources

Archives and Libraries

Basketball Hall of Fame: p. 71
Brown Brothers: pp. 18, 61, 120
Corbis-Bettmann: pp. 11, 54, 71, 77, 84, 108, 117, 131
Culver Pictures: p. 21
Frank Driggs Collection: pp. 24, 59, 83, 125
George Eastman House: p. 22
Library of Congress: pp. 10, 16, 98, 129, 130
Costas Machlouzarides: p. 109
Morris-Jumel Mansion: pp. 114, 118
Museum of the City of New York: pp. 8, 43, 94, 105, 110
National Academy of Design: p. 95
New-York Historical Society: pp. 14, 25, 33, 90, 98, 121
New York Public Library, Astor, Lenox and Tilden Foundations,
    Schomburg Center for Research in Black Culture: pp. 27, 28, 56,
    75, 88, 99, 113, 122, 124, 127 Austin Hansen Collection: pp. 87,
    126
    Library for the Performing Arts, Billy Rose Theater Collection: p. 63
    United States History, Local History and Genealogy Division: pp.
    36, 42, 47, 49, 51, 66, 74, 100, 107, 111
Office of Metropolitan History: pp. 60, 72
Donna Van Der Zee: pp. 37, 80, 86

Publications

American Architect and Building News: p. 41 (April 12, 1890)
Architectural Era: p. 110 (February 1890)
Architectural Record: p. 96 (April 1907)
Henry Collins Brown, ed. *Valentine's Manual of the City of New*
    York (1918-19): p. 44
Churchman: p. 92 (December 5, 1891)
National Terra Cotta Society, Architectural Terra Cotta Brochure
    Series, "The Theater 2": p. 123
Real Estate Record and Builders Guide: p. 12 (November 7, 1891),
    p. 38 (June 22, 1891), p. 39 (January 23, 1892),
    p. 45 (September 7, 1892), p. 67 (September 17, 1892),
    p. 73 (April 9, 1892), p. 81 (April 9, 1982),
    p. 91 (September 13, 1890), p. 104 (March 25, 1893)
Scientific American Architects and Builders Edition: p. 102
D.H. Valentine, *Manual of the Corporation of the City of New*
    York (1856): p. 7

Index to Tours